Sensing Software Evolution

Software exploration with audio-tactile cognitive visualization

Dissertation

for the Degree of a
Doctor in Informatics

at the Faculty of Economics
Business Administration and
Information Technology
of the University of Zurich

by
Sandro Boccuzzo

from
Zurich, Switzerland

under supervision of
Prof. Dr. Harald C. Gall

March 2012

Sensing Software Evolution
Sandro Boccuzzo
Copyright © 2012 by Sandro Boccuzzo

ISBN 978-1-291-08951-6 (Paperback - Color)
ISBN 978-1-291-09026-0 (Paperback - Black and White)
ISBN 978-1-291-09023-9 (E-Book)

The Faculty of Economics, Business Administration and Information Technology of the University of Zurich herewith permits the publication of the aforementioned dissertation without expressing any opinion on the views contained therein.

Zurich, March 2012

Head of the Ph.D. committee for informatics:

Prof. Abraham Bernstein, PhD.

Dissertation accepted on March, 2012

Accepted on the recommendation of

Prof. Dr. Harald C. Gall
University of Zurich, Switzerland
Advisor

Prof. Dr. Michele Lanza
University of Lugano, Switzerland
Second Advisor

Acknowledgments

When I started my doctoral studies, I never would have guessed so many people would contribute in some sort to writing this dissertation. From discussions within the research groups, coffee breaks, bachelor and master students up to endless discussions with researchers during and after international conferences. I am grateful for all their valuable input. First and most important I would like to thank my advisor, Harald C. Gall, for his great support in endless directions. He not only had an open door, whenever I needed an advice. Thanks to his great effort in writing the project proposals this work was made possible in the first place. Over the years he told me what to pay attention to when writing papers, how to have fun in research and not to do everything at the last minute. Still, in the end he found tolerance when a paper was there to be submitted again at the very last minute. I thank him as well for supporting my extravagant PhD lifestyle with compassion. Especially when submitting the paper for WCRE 2007 from a youth hostel in a Canadian national park, the paper for ISCM 2008 from the carneval in Brazil, or from letting me getting back from ICSM Beijing with the Trans-Siberian train. He knew that a conference for me meant always research talks combined with a lot of incredible extra stuff. Last but not least I thank him for his extra support during the last year to get this work to an end.

I thank Michele Lanza for all his valuable input during these years. He offered a great support, with refreshing ideas during several, sometimes exhausting Evospaces project meetings. I thank him for inviting us to sunny Lugano, whenever an extra motivated effort was required and for the unforgettable time spent with him at conferences. I especially remember his advices at the lunch to celebrate the end of the Evospaces project and the discussions I had with him at the MSA 2010 in Locarno. Unforgettable remains the surprise in his face when I showed up at ICSE 2010 in South Africa and he found out what I had already been doing in the three previous days. And I will not forget his exquisite wine taste at conference dinners.

My thanks goes to the other members of the Evospaces project Philippe Dugerdil,

Sazzadul Alam, and Richard Wettel for the great effort they have been putting towards the combined project and their discussions towards implementing the aural-tactile visual approaches. Many thanks goes to the Hasler Foundation Switzerland for supporting my dissertation over these years within the Projects "EvoSpaces I/II". Nothing would have been possible without the extraordinary great seal group. If I just think of all the extra hours Michael Wuersch, Matthias Hert and Amancio Bouza used to correct once again one of my error prone first draft conference papers. My thanks goes to Martin Pinzger and Michael Fischer for their great support when I started my research. They really were helpful in getting this project towards promising directions. Geri Reif for all his assistance and the fun time when we shared a room at the university. Emanuel Giger for explaining to me basic statistics and latent semantic indexing over and over again and for taking me to new horizons with the snow kite. Beat Fluri for all his advices towards my research, his typography wisdom sharing for the design of this final document and not least for taking me on a cross-country skiing tour across Basel downtown during carneval. Patrick Knab for the great time we spent together at the university and for his effort towards pushing me to get my license to play on golf courses. I further thank Giacomo Ghezzi and Yi Guo for all their precious time they gently offered with regard to my thesis.

Many grateful thanks go to Serge Demeyer for sharing his ideas on my work while on a sabbatical leave in our lab, and for all his advices with regard to writing a thesis. I personally appreciate his constant offer to read my work.

Special thanks goes to Lucia Horvath for her effort concerning the evaluation of the survey.

Grateful thanks goes to Patrizia Milz, Stephan Gerhard, Franziska Spring, Tom Philip, Tonya Walder, and Daniel Walder for all the time spent in reviewing and correcting my work.

My greatest appreciation go to Adriana, Laszlo and Carolina Horvath for their effort in supporting me when I needed it the most.

My special dedicated thanks goes to my parents Silvia and Salvatore and my brother Remo, who for all my life keep believing in what I am capable of and for remaining calm during the last year where not always a clear path showed that finally a doctoral degree would arise out from this endless work. I thank you so much. This work is dedicated to you.

SANDRO BOCCUZZO

University of Zurich, Switzerland
March 2012

to Lucia's and my family

Abstract

As software evolves, it increases in size, it undergoes many changes and becomes more and more complex such that it gets hard to comprehend it. To understand this abstract manner of software, research has attempted to simplify the understanding. One form of simplifying the understanding is to visualize software. Over the years, research in software visualization brought various solutions to address a software's complexity. Some visualizations used hierarchies and showed the packages, classes and methods to get an understanding of a software's structure. Others calculated metrics out of changes, hierarchies and relations of entities and present the software in a problem-oriented way. We focus on improving the perception of software in our first step. Our general approach is to use objects known from our daily life such as the simple shape of a house to represent software components. The so-called glyphs are shaped based on the characteristics of the software components they represent. Because human observers know from their daily life how the glyph should look like, they recognize well-formed proportions of houses, e.g. roof versus body of the house. The perception can therefore be improved by visualizing the software according to an observer's knowledge.

Based on this general idea of improving perception of software when using an observer's knowledge, we focus on further aspects. We present audio as a means to support a visualization in the same way we experience a movie more intense if supported with a sound track. In our work, we used an aural feedback to get a fast glimpse on other secondary characteristics of a visualized software component and researched how the use of audio feedback combined with sound technologies allow to guide an observer towards interesting aspects in a visualization.

On top of this audio-visual approach, we looked for a simplification to access software visualization in general. With a focus on tasks engineers commonly use during their daily maintenance work, we implemented a framework to automate the configuration processes for a software visualization.

We combined the approaches with tactile navigation on multitouch devices. This offered an observer access to explore a software with more natural behavior, similar as moving objects such as a glass or a paper around a table.

My research thesis is as follows: Visualizing evolving source code in a comprehensive understandable form provides insights to existing and emerging problems and supports finding relevant aspects with adequate tactile interaction and aural feedback.

In the end, we opened the horizon to possibilities of improving multitouch navigation with simple spoken commands and looked at the opportunities that our approach offers for the collaboration among software engineers involved in the team. The main contribution of this dissertation is CoCoViz, a methodology and tool to support an engineer in understanding an evolving software system with the help of an observer's senses and his present knowledge. Multi-Touch screen technology combined with an audio supported 3D software visualization offers a promising way for the software engineers involved in a project to understand a software system and share knowledge about it in an intuitive manner. We validated our methodology with a survey addressing the different aspects of our approach. The main advantages of our methodology can be summarized as follows:

1. *Cognitive perception of virtual entities.* With our approach we can match virtual entities to familiar natural objects. Compared to the state-of-the-art a perception of data is facilitated as the observer already is familiar with the used metaphors.

2. *Guided analysis of data.* To analyze a software visualization other approaches often require a second visualization. When using audio on top of a visualization an observer can address the audio to support the visual impression and preserve the focus on the primer software visualization.

3. *Intuitive collaboration.* Current visualizations are often not intuitive because controls within the visualization and the capabilities to share information limit an observer's workflow. In a multi-touch environment we can arrange the access to adequate controls in an intuitive and natural way and leverage the multiuser capabilities of tactile devices together with information sharing approaches.

Zusammenfassung

Eine Software Architektur entwickelt sich über die Zeit. Dabei verändert sich die Architektur oft so stark, dass es schwierig wird für den Einzelnen diese ganz zu verstehen. Um den abstrakten Sachverhalt von Software besser zu verstehen, versucht die Forschung das Verständnis zu vereinfachen. Eine Art, dieses Verständnis zu vereinfachen ist Software zu visualisieren. Über die Jahre haben Forscher verschiedene Lösungen für Software Visualisierungen präsentiert. Einige nutzen die Hierarchie und veranschaulichen die Softwarestruktur mit dem Zeigen von Paketen, Klassen und Methoden. Andere berechnen Metriken aus Veränderungen, Hierarchien und Relationen und präsentieren Software in einer problemorientierten Weise. Am Ende versuchen aber alle Software Visualisierungen darauf, die Wahrnehmung des aktuellen Softwaresystems zu verbessern.

Im ersten Teil der Arbeit befassen wir uns mit der verbesserten Wahrnehmung von Software Systemen. Unser grundlegender Ansatz ist, Gegenstände aus unserem täglichen Leben, wie die Formen eines einfachen Hauses zu verwenden und mit ihnen Softwarekomponenten darzustellen. Diese Objekte werden gemäss den Charakteristiken der gezeigten Softwarekomponenten geformt. Weil ein Betrachter die Gegenstände aus dem täglichen Leben kennt und weiss wie Sie aussehen sollten, erkennt er Unterschiede wie ein kleines Dach verglichen zum Basiskörper sehr schnell. Die Wahrnehmung wird darin verbessert, dass Software unter der Verwendung des Grundwissens des Betrachters visualisiert wird.

Basierend auf der grundlegenden Idee die Wahrnehmung von Software durch die Verwendung vom Grundwissen des Betrachters zu verbessern, haben wir andere verwandte Aspekte betrachtet. Wir verwenden Audio als eine Form Softwarevisualisierung zu unterstützen, in ähnlicher Weise wie eine Tonspur die Wahrnehmung eines Films unterstützt. In unserer Arbeit ermöglicht Audio einen schnellen Einblick über sekundäre Charakteren der visualisierten Softwarekomponente.

Wir forschten des weiteren in wiefern eine Audio Rückmeldung kombiniert mit Surround-Sound Technologie dazu verwendet werden kann, einen Betrachter zu interessanten Aspekten in der Software Visualisierung zu führen. Aufbauend auf dem audio-visuellen Ansatz befassten wir uns damit, wie der Einstieg in die Verwendung von Softwarevisualisierung vereinfacht werden kann. Wir fokussierten dabei auf übliche Arbeitsschritte, welche Softwareentwickler während ihrer täglichen Arbeit verwenden. Darauf aufbauend erstellten wir ein System, welches das Automatisieren der Konfigurationsprozesse für eine Software Visualisierung weitgehend automatisiert.

Wir kombinierten unsere Ansätze mit einer taktilen Navigation auf Multitouchgeräten. Dies erlaubt es dem Betrachter ein visualisiertes Softwareprojekt mit einer natürlichen Handhabung zu erforschen, fast so wie das verschieben eines Glases oder eines Papiers auf einem Tisch. Wir erweiterten unseren Horizont dahin, dass wir mit einfachen verbalen Befehlen diese taktile Navigation in gewissen Situationen verbessern konnten. Am Schluss der Arbeit betrachteten wir die Möglichkeiten, welche unsere Ansätze für die Förderung der Zusammenarbeit zwischen beteiligten Softwareentwicklern anbieten.

Als Hauptbeitrag dieser Dissertation präsentieren wir COCOVIZ, eine Methodik zur Verständnisunterstützung eines wandelnden Software Systems. Multi-Touch Technologien kombiniert mit audio-unterstützter 3D Software Visualisation ermöglicht es Softwareentwicklern ein Software Projekt zu verstehen und Informationen und Wissen über dieses System intuitiv unter den Beteiligten auszutauschen. Wir überprüfen unseren Ansatz mit einer Umfrage, welche die verschiedenen Teilaspekte unseres Ansatzes in Betracht zieht. Die Hauptvorteile unseres Ansatzes finden sich im speziellen in:

1. *Kognitiven Wahrnehmung von virtuellen Komponenten.* Mit unserem Ansatz können wir virtuelle Komponenten mit uns vertrauten natürlichen Objekten verknüpfen. Im Vergleich zu anderen Ansätzen wird die Wahrnehmung von Daten dadurch vereinfacht, da dem Beobachter die verwendeten Metaphern bereits vertraut sind.

2. *Unterstützte Analyse von Daten.* Um Software über einen bestimmten Punkt hinweg analysieren zu können, wird in bestehenden Ansätzen oft das Erstellen von mehreren verschiedenen Visualisierungen unabdingbar. In dem wir eine Visualisierung zusätzlich mit Audio ergänzen, können wir einen Betrachter in seiner visuellen Wahrnehmung unterstützen. Dadurch können wir auch verhindern, dass dieser seinen Hauptfokus in der Software Visualisierung verliert.

3. *Intuitive Kollaboration.* Bestehende Visualisierungen sind oft nicht intuitiv genug, weil deren Bedienelemente und die Fähigkeiten die Informationen zu teilen den Betrachter limitieren. In einer Multi-touch Umgebung können wir den Zugriff auf geeignete Bedienelemente in einer intuitiven Form ermöglichen. Zusätzlich können wir die Kollaborationsmöglichkeiten solcher Umgebungen mit Fähigkeiten die Informationen mit anderen Mitarbeitern zu teilen verknüpfen.

Contents

II Approach   31

III Evaluation   97

IV Retrospection 143

11 Contributions to Software Engineering 145

V Closing 151

12 Conclusion 153

VI Appendix 157

A Evaluation Questionnaire 159

B Glossary 177

C Publications 179

Bibliography 181

Curriculum Vitae 192

Figures

Tables

Part I
Prologue

Prologue

1

Introduction

1.1 Motivation

Vision is one of the most relevant exteroceptive senses. With our eyes we perceive millions of changes and process information within seconds. For decades, humans have been sharing information aurally. Finally, mankind started to collect information by visualizing it. Cave men paintings, such as the ones in South Africa's Drakensberg have preserved such information over centuries. Ancient Egyptians with their hieroglyphs used a combination of logographic and alphabetical elements to pass on information and the Romans relied on seven symbols only to visualize statistical information. The Roman numeral system is still used in science to categorize stages such as for embryos and larvae stages [Gos60] or to categorize collagen genes in the biological sciences [VDC90].

When it comes to visualizing statistical information, the work of Edward Tufte has been seminal, who in the mid 70's developed a set of lectures on statistical graphics. His work was later published in the book *The Visual Display of Quantitative Information* [TH99] and is still regarded as a foundation for presentation of informational graphics.

When we look at visualizing software, most of the approaches used today simply represent the system as squares such as Johnson and Shneidermann's Tree maps [JS91], or some form of pie charts or stars as in Pinzger *et al.*'s ArchView [PGFL05]. Looking at these approaches we learn that even if all these approaches deal with presenting the information in a comprehensive way, it is often hard to understand the relevant aspects right away or to compare two components with each other.

Two simple pie charts shall serve for illustration purposes (Figure 1.1). How would you compare the two pie charts, if you did not know anything about the underlying data? Even though the two charts are visualized in a simple and understandable

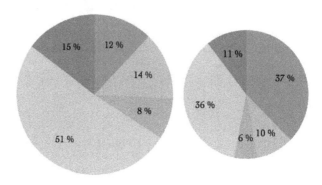

Figure 1.1: Which of the two pie charts is more relevant?

manner, it is hard to compare them without any knowledge of the underlying data. Now, if you think of them as two pie charts representing the same entity in two different time periods, would you state the changes to be representative of an improvement or rather as a deterioration of the entity? In our view, a visualization should allow for a first discussion about a general situation even when knowing only the semantics of the data and not the underlying data in detail. Our first research question, therefore, is:

How can an evolving software system be visualized in a comprehensive and understandable manner?

Evaluating today's state-of-the-art in software visualization reveals that a variety of approaches are being applied. These range from Lanza and Ducasse's Polymetric Views [LD02] to Inselber and Dimsdale's Parallel Coordinates [ID90]. They represent two kinds of approaches, those that focus more on a software project's hierarchy or those that focus more on metric measurements and analysis. Still, only few companies use software visualizations in practice. Engineers tend to avoid using software visualization in a productive software development process. A possible reason may be the initial effort needed to learn how to configure and use software visualization compared to the expected benefit arising from its use. Unless an engineer sees a clear benefit, he most probably will not take any steps into visualization. Another reason for not using any visualization can be seen in its construction that often is not intuitive enough and sometimes complicated. We suggest that the step to configure an adequate visualization needs to be facilitated at least for the most common use cases in order to simplify the use of software visualization. Our second research question is:

How can the effort needed to configure a software visualization be decreased?

Visualizing data in a comprehensive and understandable manner is a desirable solution, however, what happens with the visualization afterwards must also be considered. Let us concentrate on the purpose of a visualization. A visualization is used to simplify the perception of data. Complex relations are combined to facilitate the understanding. Still, in the end an observer will have to interpret the visualization. Most of today's visualizations for software projects focus on how to visualize the domain's complex aspects. However, the interpretation is completely left to the observer. This is problematic whenever the complexity is not dissolved completely. In such a case, the interpretation may not be facilitated by the visualization. In the end an engineer is interested in finding what is of relevance to him in a software project and he needs support for that. Our third research question is:

How can finding relevant aspects in (software) visualizations be supported?
Finding relevant aspects is an important part. What if the findings are not in an engineer's responsibility anymore? An engineer will need to consult others. The more complex a system gets, the more often a solution for a problem does not concern only one engineer. A visualization has to allow for communication between the involved parties. To support such discussions and decision making the interaction and navigation in a visualization an important. Our fourth research question is:

How can we support navigation and interaction in software visualizations?
We claim that in using common metaphors to visualize software entities we can improve the general comprehension of a software project. We claim further that we can lower the threshold to use a software visualization in development, by automating the configuration for the most common use case and software engineering questions.

In supporting the visualization with adequate aural feedback we can sustain an engineer's interpretation and guide him to relevant aspects.

In adapting multitouch techniques we allow engineers to discuss and interpret a visualized software project in a user-friendly manner, enforcing communication and collaboration among engineers from different domains of responsibility.

We state the following thesis:

Visualizing evolving source code in a comprehensive understandable form provides insights to existing and emerging problems and supports observers in finding relevant aspects with adequate tactile interaction and aural feedback.

1.2 Visualizing with CocoViz

In this dissertation, we present COCOVIZ, an approach to visualize evolving software projects. This approach allows one to combine software metrics from different domains, to use filters according to a particular situation and to present software entities adequately. Most common software metrics are supported and the importer offers a framework to extend these metrics with other data. The format to describe software entities is based on Demeyer *et al.*'s language independent meta-model called Famix [DTP99]. The COCOVIZ data model comprises two major components. One component includes the analyzed software project, its entities and hierarchies and the other the mapping to the visual representations. An engineer can directly adjust the mappings to adapt the visualization according to his interest. The adjusted mappings are used to calculate a software entity's shape, color, texture and location. To facilitate perception and to allow a general comparison, these software entities are represented as objects known from our daily life (*e. g.* a house). COCOVIZ offers a variety of algorithms to adjust the way the color, texture and location of an entity is calculated.

Our approach can be considered dynamic in that the calculated visualization is a non static image. An observer is constantly navigating in a three-dimensional visualization and explores the present system dynamically. To support him in finding relevant aspects we extended the visualization with aural feedback. In COCOVIZ an active triggered aural feedback (entity audio) and a passive aural feedback are used (ambient audio).

To lower the configuration effort, preconfigured templates (comprehension tasks) for common use cases are applied. A framework allows to extend these preconfigured templates according to the engineer's needs.

To exploit the benefits of having engineers get together and discuss a software project, COCOVIZ was adapted for the use on multitouch tables during software reviews.

In this work, we present a user study addressing several concepts of our approach. The results provide evidence that the COCOVIZ approach contributes to the understanding of a software system.

1.3 Research Hypotheses

We base the verification of this thesis on the acceptance of four main hypotheses, which are further specified in detailed hypotheses. A general position of our work is that human understanding can be optimized if a dataset is adequately presented. Our idea to map measurements to objects with a cognitive meaning is supported by related work such as Chernoff's faces [Che73].

We base this work on the general hypothesis: Cognitive metaphors contribute to human understanding. Cognitive sciences have been investigating how human perception is processed and how it affects reasoning and emotional states. Work in the field of artificial intelligence regarding neural networks and embodiment give possible explanations on how data are processed and how important it is to see the processing as a form of adaption of an individuum to its environment [PMI07].
Neuroscience has been studying what amenities provoke activities in certain parts of our brain [SKCC10]. In showing pictures of different situations neural activity is triggered.
Psychologists use metaphors to explain certain human behaviors and emotions. [LK97, LJ80]
All in all, there is an understanding among scientists of various fields that cognitive perceptual metaphors can facilitate the human understanding of a given situation.

HYPOTHESIS 1: Cognitive metaphors can be used for software exploration.

Hypothesis 1a: Software metrics (SM) mapped to objects known from our daily lives allow an effective categorization of the underlying software entity.
Software metrics describe a characteristic of a program component. These metrics can be used to define, the widths and lengths of polygons. Out of polygons, for example, familiar objects can be built such as a simple house made from a cube and a pyramid on top. Different metrics therefore affect the size and shape of an object and thus allow differentiating between such objects. With an useful set of metrics (metric cluster) and an optimized scaling, the distinguishable objects allow an effective categorization of the underlying software entity.
We verify this hypothesis with respect to object-oriented software projects, in a user study. In addition, we present a prototype implementing the described concepts.

Hypothesis 1b: Software metrics mapped to objects known from our daily lives allow for a comparison of the underlying software entity, even without detailed knowledge of the underlying mapping.
We assume that engineers involved in analyzing software might not know all the details of the current software project. Our proposed mapping to known objects allows engineers to compare entities and discuss them in general without being aware of all the details.
We verify this hypothesis with a user study that compares similar and different objects and their underlying software entity. In addition, we present a prototype that implements the described concepts.

HYPOTHESIS 2: Sound can be used to support visual software exploration.

Hypothesis 2a: Software metrics mapped to the pitch and tune of a sound sample permit an accurate categorization of the underlying software entity.
Music and sound are important parts of human perception. We note that most contemporary movies have an audio track to support the visual impression. It comes without saying that audio has an influence on our perception. With software metrics mapped to the pitch and tone of a sound sample we can bring similar characteristics to software exploration and support a visual perception.
We verify this hypothesis with respect to object-oriented software projects and a user study. In addition, we present a prototype implementing the described concepts.

Hypothesis 2b: Software metrics mapped to the pitch and tone of a sound sample permit an accurate perception of the evolutionary changes in the underlying software entity.
A tone difference of a sound is easily perceptible [ZFH01]. Mapping software metrics to the pitch and tone of a sound sample allows listening to a characteristic of a program component. Combining the sound sample of one component over its evolving stage constructs a music sequence representing the history of that program component.
With an ideal set of metrics (metric cluster) and an optimized scaling of the metric deltas from one version to another the sequence allows aural perception of the underlying software entity's history.
We verify this hypothesis with respect to an object-oriented software project in an user study. In addition, we present a prototype implementing the described concepts.

Hypothesis 2c: In a three dimensional visualization with surround sound, an observer is guided to a specific position in that visualization by simultaneously emitting adequate sound samples from the position of the underlying mapped software entity.
Software metrics are mapped to the pitch and tune of a sound sample. The sounds are then linked to the position of an object in the visualization. An extra object is used to represent the position of the observer. With the use of a surround sound algorithm we calculate the sound the observer would listen to at the current position. This approach allows us to use the sound type and its volume to lead an observer to a specific location.
We use our prototype to verify this hypothesis with respect to an object-oriented software project and verify its applicability with an user study.

Hypothesis 2d: Using a three dimensional visualization with surround sound, together with a force-directed layout algorithm, allows for a prediction of the stability of interconnected software entities.
We assume that the linking of sounds to the location of a visualized object can enable detection of complex relation. If we use a force directed graph as a layout algorithm for the visualization, stronger related objects move closer together in the visualization. In generating sound samples from mapped metrics linked to these related objects would enforce a stronger sound perception and allow us conclusions about the stability of software entity groups.
This hypothesis is verified with respect to object-oriented software projects in combination with related work.

HYPOTHESIS 3: Tactile interfaces can be used to support the interaction during software exploration.

Hypothesis 3a: Multi-touch gestures mapped to navigation and interaction commands enable an adequate exploration of a software visualization.
Navigation in a software exploration uses zooming, rotating, moving objects, filtering entities and requesting aural feedback. We show that an adequate software exploration is possible in using a set of gestures on a common multi-touch table.

Hypothesis 3b: Mapping navigation and interaction commands to adequate multitouch gesture permits an intuitive exploration in a three dimensional software visualization with minimal introduction overhead.
We assume that navigation in a software exploration is possible on a common multitouch table. In mapping the gestures to intuitively expected commands the navigation is simplified and thus a minimal introduction is needed for new users.

We perform an user study to identify expected commands for specific gestures and our prototype to verify the mappings with respect to an object-oriented software project.

HYPOTHESIS 4: Speech can be used to enhance the interaction on tactile interfaces during software exploration.

Hypothesis 4a: Using spoken commands in combination with gestures in software exploration on a multitouch table permits to lower the need to access a keyboard and to speed up a task.
We show that navigation in a software exploration is possible on a multi-touch table. Still most common use cases are not limited to navigation and afford selection, search or changing tasks. In using spoken commands in combination to the multi-touch gesture navigation we enable a smoother workflow and limit the need to access a multi-touch keyboard.
In our current methodology speech is considered an add-on to our tactile approach. This hypothesis therefore is verified only as part of the case study in Chapter 7.

1.4 Research Goals

For our research we considered a number of research goals.

COGNITIVE GLYPHS

Research Goal 1: Create cognitive glyphs that enable intuitive understanding of the underlying data.
The goal relies on hypothesis H1a and H1b. A cognitive glyph has to be commonly understandable and still the glyphs have to be distinguishable among each other. Furthermore, the glyphs have to reflect whether two glyphs are similar or different in their characteristics to ensure acceptance of H1b.

AURAL FEEDBACK

Research Goal 2: Create aural feedback that enables intuitive understanding of the underlying data set.
Audio is intended to support a visual exploration. To achieve this, an aural feedback is required that is commonly understood and that avoids misinterpretation. In fulfilling this goal we address H2a. If we can create an aural feedback composed of a sequence of sound samples and still maintain the common understandability we can accept H2b.

Research Goal 3: Create sound sample that enables to guide an engineer in three dimensional context with surround sound.
The perception and the reaction to an aural feedback is important for this research goal. The goal relates to H2c and H2d. In providing evidence that a sound sample can guide an engineer in a three dimensional context we assure the usefulness of aural feedback not only for the purpose of analysis but also for providing suggestive feedback. In solving this goal we can show that aural feedback is useful to solve more complex situations, with regard to H2d.

INTUITIVE NAVIGATION

Research Goal 4: Define gestures that enable intuitive navigation and software exploration.
Visual navigation depends on interaction. The more intuitive we can provide the experience, the less introduction is needed. Thus the visual solution finding becomes more efficient. In answering this goal we adhere to H3a and H3b.

Research Goal 5: Create configurations to automate the creation of an initial visualization for common engineering tasks to limit the typical costs of using software exploration.
Software exploration offers a simple and understandable way to look at a software project. The creation of a visualization is costly. If the effort to create such a visualization is immense, an observer might not use visualization at all. With this research goal we address possibilities to limit the effort used for creation and improve acceptance to use software exploration during common tasks.

Research Goal 6: Define spoken commands that permit to solve a task on a multitouch table, and speeding up the task itself.
Multi-touch tables are convenient for a visual navigation. Often though software exploration involves not only visual actions to solve the task, some further configuration or searching is needed. On a multi-touch table the access to a virtual keyboard is inconvenient. With adequate spoken commands we can address this situation and limit the need to access a virtual keyboard on a multi-touch table. In answering this goal we adhere to H4a.

1.5 Foundation of the Dissertation

The foundation of this dissertation is a set of selected publications. In the following, we summarize the main contributions to design an intuitive software exploration with suggestive feedback.

1. We described initial considerations on how to design intuitive software visualizations and the concept of using cognitive glyphs to enable simplified understanding of software projects [BG07b].

2. We endorse our initial concepts with a first prototype presenting software entities as cognitive glyphs [BG07a].

3. We presented concepts to directly access further details in a software exploration with aural feedback [BG08].

4. On top of that, we modified the approach to a more suggestive aural feedback guiding an observer towards the points of interests [BG09b].

5. We presented an initial approach to simplify the configuration and steps needed to access a visual software exploration with our concepts of automated tasks [BG09a].

6. Next, we focused on using emerging technologies to improve navigation and interaction, where we presented initial results [BG10].

1.6 Contribution

The conceptual contribution of the thesis is *a methodology for intuitive software exploration* that we CoCoViz. This methodology addresses concepts for a simplified creation of a software visualization. It incorporates several concepts. One of the main concepts builds on the idea of using cognitive glyphs to provide intuitive perception of the underlying data. Another key concept explains how to support an observer in the interaction with such a visualization using aural feedback to provide access to further details. An extension to this concept uses aural feedback as a recommender feedback capable to guide an observer towards points of interest.
The technical contribution consists in the creation of a tool to explore a software project in an intuitive manner. It incorporates a center component addressing mapping and filtering to enable an interactive exploration experience. On top of that, the architecture allows for the selection of cognitive glyphs as well as color-, layout- and aural-feedback algorithms. The tool is compatible to run on multi-touch devices (e.g. multi-touch screens, or even Smartphones) to endorse one or more observers with an optimal intuitive navigation.

The main contributions of this dissertation are the following:

1. A simple to understand cognitively enriched visualization to understand, explain and analyze software projects.

2. A methodology to 1) map a set of software metrics to cognitive glyphs. 2) map software metrics with audio sources and provide aural feedback. 3) guide an observer during software exploration with aural feedback.

3. A framework to 1) semi-automate the configuration processes needed to create a visual software exploration. 2) adapt software exploration to emerging multi-touch technologies.

4. An approach that addresses the collaborative workflow around common software comprehension tasks.

5. COCOVIZ, an integrated tool that implements all the concepts mentioned above.

1.7 Overview of the thesis

The remainder of this dissertation consists of the following parts:

Chapter 2 (p.15) gives an overview on related work in software visualization, as well as the use of audio and multitouch in software engineering.

Chapter 3 (p.33) describes our general COCOVIZ approach. We show the key concepts of visualizing and interacting with a dataset and explain the underlying architecture.

Chapter 4 (p.47) presents the concept of supporting a software visualization with audio. We present two approaches of mapping an audio source to entities and discuss in the situations where benefits of using an audio support arises.

Chapter 5 (p.63) introduces the concept of automated tasks. We discuss the basic concepts and how these tasks can lower the configuration effort to create a software visualization.

Chapter 6 (p.73) describes the use of multitouch-technologies in conjunction with COCOVIZ visual and aural concepts. We describe the used technologies and discuss use cases where this combination improves interaction.

Chapter 7 (p.85) presents a solution to combine multitouch-technologies with spoken commands to overcome the need of a keyboard and mouse in some situations.

Chapter 8 (p.89) discusses opportunity to leverage the benefits of software visualization in a collaborative environment.

Chapter 9 (p.101) discusses the design of our survey.

Chapter 10 (p.107) shows the results of our survey with regard to our hypothesis.

Chapter 11 (p.145) discusses our contributions to software visualization. We present to what extent our approach contributes to the understanding of software evolution and supports software exploration.

Chapter 12 (p.153) presents conclusions and outlines future work.

Appendix A (p.159) presents the evaluation questionnaire used during our user study.

Appendix B (p.177) gives a glossary with regard to this work.

Appendix C (p.179) presents selected publications.

2

Related Work

Software visualization is an important part of software engineering when it comes to understand complexity and address the topic of abstraction. In the early nineties attempts were made to visualize the software's tree structures such as Johnson and Shneidermanns treemaps [JS91], the focus residing more on efficient presentation than understanding.

Eick's Seesoft on the other hand drew more attention to the statistics, by coloring the software components based on changes to the characteristics of interest [ESS92]. In order to understand software, we have to consider more than just visualizing characters. When to use software visualization and how to interpret, explore, and work on the results is just as important. To stress this dynamic software visualization will be referred to as software exploration throughout this work.

Software exploration not only refers to the presentation of the abstract characteristics of software in an understandable form, it most importantly underlines the importance on the interaction, and analysis of the presentation. The goal is to gather conclusions from the software's representation. Therefore, software exploration should not be regarded as limited to a visual preparation of the underlying data, but rather as a combination of several forms of interactions.

This chapter gives an overview of the state-of-the-art related to this work. The remainder is structured as follows: In Section 2.1 we present some relevant approaches in software visualization. Section 2.2 shows work done in cognitive object comprehension. Section 2.3 offers an overview on work related to audio support. In Section 2.4 we deal with work related to our automated tasks approach. Section 2.5 concerns related work to interaction with software visualization with regard to the use of tactile devices. Section 2.6 opens the overview to related work in collaboration on software projects and Section 2.7 concludes with a résumé on how CoCoViz uses and extends these previous approaches.

2.1 Software Visualization

As mentioned in the introduction to this section software visualization aims to visually represent the complex context of software projects. However, visualization is not only a discipline used for software. It is rather understood as a means for scientists and engineers to access collections of data and to get insights on the data. With the increasing amount of features in a software project and the customer's demand to run on several platforms at the same time, the complexity and the amount of information that needs to be understood becomes hardly manageable. For a successful project preserving an accurate overview is crucial. Project analysis, preparation and an adequate visual presentation of the data are important factors for a successful project. In the past few years a variety of approaches dedicated to software visualization and software reengineering emerged. Most of the visualization methods use a graphical representation of data rendered either in a two-dimensional or three-dimensional view. The visualizations can roughly be categorized into two main categories that differ in their means a project is focused: Hierarchical visualization and metrics visualization.

2.1.1 Hierarchical visualization

Hierarchical visualization approaches attempt to display large hierarchies in a comprehensible manner. The visualization often allows a quick overview on the whole project. Johnson and Shneidermann are among the first to gather numerous acceptance with their approach. With treemaps they proposed to map tree structures on to rectangular regions [JS91]. The efficient use of space allows to display very large hierarchies with thousands of leaves, while still being comprehensible (Figure 2.1 left). A drawback of this approach is however, the decreasing readability of very large hierarchies and the limited comparability of similar software components on different hierarchy levels.

Unlike Johnson and Shneidermann, Robertson *et al.* [RMC91] - in their work on Cone Trees - laid out the hierarchy in a three-dimensional manner, where the children of a node are placed evenly spaced along a cone base. Through rotation of the cone base a viewer can bring different parts of the tree into focus (Figure 2.1 right). A major criticism on this approach is however the difficulty to manipulate larger tree structures. In their work, they showed that Cone Trees with more than 1000 nodes are difficult to manipulate [LRP95]. Therefore, Cone Trees might be considered for medium-sized trees only.

A rather interesting approach is drawn in [DE01]. In their work, Dachselt and Ebert recommend an interaction technique for medium-sized trees: The Collapsi-

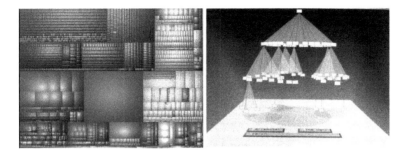

Figure 2.1: Program visualization with Treemap [JS91] and Cone Trees [RMC91]

ble Cylindrical Trees (CCT). A CCT maps the child nodes on a rotating cylinder (Figure 2.2). In doing so the hierarchical structure is addressed in a fast and intuitive manner and allows one to dynamically hide or show further details. The uniqueness of this work is seen in that compared to most other work in the field of hierarchical views they do not concentrate on how to display large hierarchies in a comprehensible manner but rather on the interaction of the engineer with the data itself. Their work shows the importance of user-data interaction as a main criteria for an intuitive software visualization.

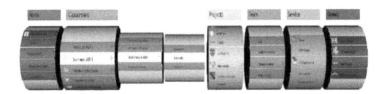

Figure 2.2: Program visualization with Collapsible Cylindrical Trees [DE01]

Yang *et al.* with InterRing propose an interactive approach for navigating and manipulating hierarchical structures [YWR02b]. Their tool visualizes the hierarchy with radial, space-filling (RSF) techniques (Figure 2.3 left). They state that RSF offers several advantages over traditional node-link diagrams, with regard to efficient display space usage. In their work they also describe how with InterRing they can perform significantly more operations than with prior systems such as multi-focus distortions and interactive hierarchy reconfiguration.

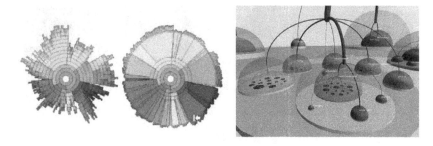

Figure 2.3: Visualization with InterRing [YWR02b] and hierarchical net [BD04]

Balzer *et al.* on the other side in [BD04] suggested the use of abstract metaphors to visualize entities in software architecture (Figure 2.3 right). Aside from the hierarchy, in their approach the entities are related to each other through inheritance, access and call relationships. The hierarchical structures are represented by nested hemispheres. For better reading and performance transparency is used to present or hide details. This allows to present larger software structures whilst preserving simplicity of interaction and understanding.

2.1.2 Metrics visualization

In contrast to hierarchical visualizations, metrics visualization approaches, do not only rely on hierarchy information. Instead, they describe a software's state or situation. Generally spoken, metrics describe a characteristic of a specific software entity. The characteristics among others can represent size, complexity, relation, or hierarchy information. The goal of these approaches is to combine metrics to meaningful aspects and present these aspects in a comprehensible form.

Eick's Seesoft [ESS92] is among the first exponents of metric visualization. In the work presented in 1992 he uses the lines of code for every software entity and maps these numbers to thin rows. The rows are then colored based on a statistic of interest, *e. g.* most recently changed, least recently changed, or locations of characters. This character specific coloring enables an user to gain a quick overview of the fragmentation of a software and to easily highlight parts of interest. Nowadays, Seesoft still is regarded as an example of how much information about a software project resides inside the number of lines of code of its entities (Figure 2.4 left).

With their graphical analyzer for software evolution (GASE), Holt and Pak (1996) proposed a look at the evolution of a software [HP96]. They used GASE to describe the architectural changes during eleven revisions of an industrial software

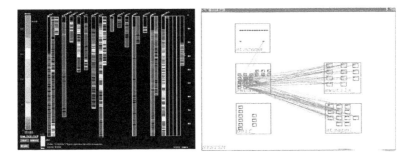

Figure 2.4: Visualization in SeeSoft [ESS92] and dependencies in GASE [HP96]

system (Figure 2.4 right). They did so in extracting relevant aspects such as modules, subsystems, calls and includes. With this information a graph is constructed representing modules as nodes and calls as edges. In the view colors are used to highlight changes from version to version.

Gall *et al.* in 1999 presented their approach for visualizing historical information [GJR99]. Similar to Holt and Pak, they use color to display historical changes to the module properties, whereas time is represented as a third dimension. In their work, 2D and 3D visual representations are explored to examine a systems's software release history (Figure 2.5 left).

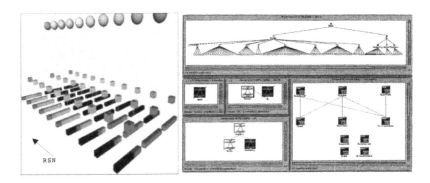

Figure 2.5: Software release history [GJR99] and SHriMP [SBM+02]

Marcus *et al.* in [MFM03] took on Eick's work and extended the Seesoft approach. They used a three-dimensional space as a representation base and mapped the metrics to height, depth, color, and position of cylinders. On top of that, several manipulation techniques were added to improve interaction.

Lanza and Ducasse contributed with their Polymetric Views [LD03], to help in understanding the structure of a software system and detect problems as early as possible in the initial phases of a reverse engineering process. In their concept they display the software entities based on their metric values as a rectangular shape. The metrics are mapped that the position, the height, the width and the color of one rectangle represents a metric value of the same software entity (Figure 2.6). This approach offers a quick overview of the softwares subdivision. Compared to Seesoft the Polymetric Views additionally include a representation of the relations within the software entities.

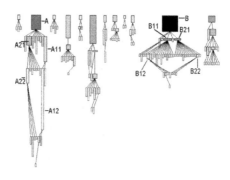

Figure 2.6: A polymetric view in CodeCrawler [LD03]

Storey *et al.* [SBM+02] focused more on the architecture level. With ShriMP (Simple Hierarchical Multi-Perspective) they suggested the use of a unified single view visualization that presents information at different levels in one visualization (Figure 2.5 right). As they state these views are suited to expose structures in larger systems. A zoom mechanism provides an alternative interaction to scroll in and out of details.

Similar to the abstract metaphor used by Balzer *et al.*, Loewe and Panas presented an architecture to analyze a model and create mappings between model and views [LP05]. Noteworthy in there approach is the concepts shown towards comprehending a programs evolution (VizzAnalyzer) and their attempt to use other metaphors to explain a model, such as a city metaphor (Figure 2.7).

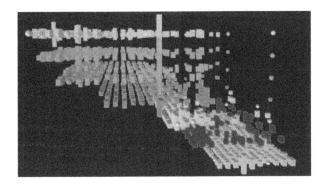

Figure 2.7: Program Evolution with VizzAnalyzer [LP05]

Various other approaches use a city metaphor to describe software entities. Noteworthy and related to this work is Wettel and Lanza's work on CodeCity [WL08] and Alam and Dugerdil's work within Evospaces [DA07].

Panas *et al.* [PEQ+07] proposed an enhanced single-view model to reduce the burden of understanding multiple views and to rapidly summarize systems. Their visualization technique unifies the presentation of various kinds of architecture-level information and offers a quick view to current developments, quality and costs of a software.

The Parallel Coordinates introduced by Inselberg and Dimsdale showed another way to visualize multi-dimensional analytic and synthetic geometry [ID90]. In a parallel coordinate view, the various metric scales are arranged vertically one after the other. For each software entity, the metric values are marked on the corresponding metric scale. A line connecting all the marks of one entity represents that software entity. This view allows to present the characters of a software entity as a footprint like representation, and offers a simple comparison of several entities.

For several years, researchers have been trying to refine the parallel coordinates to address the limitation of displaying large data sets. Fua *et al.* [FWR99] first proposed a multi-resolution view of the data. With this approach they were able to navigate through a structure by hierarchically clustering certain levels of details (Figure 2.8).

By contrast, Benedix *et al.* [BKH05] were interested in categorizing a data set. They explain how the layout of parallel coordinates can be used to visualize categorical data. They adapted the approach by substituting data points with a frequency-based representation offering auxiliary efficient work with meta-data. Johansson *et*

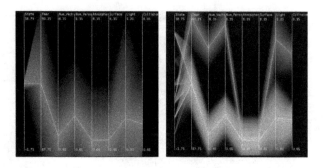

Figure 2.8: Multi-resolution view with Hierarchical Parallel Coordinates [FWR99]

al. [JCJ05] extended the standard parallel coordinates to the third dimension. In their Clustered Multi-Relational Parallel Coordinates (CMRPC) they introduced a technique to simultaneously show one-to-one relation analysis between a selected and the other dimensions (Figure 2.9).

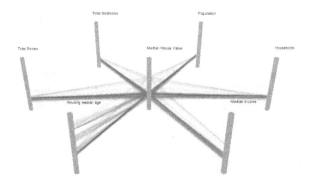

Figure 2.9: Visualization in clustered multi-relational parallel coordinates [JCJ05]

A slightly different approach was presented by Fanea *et al.* in their work on Star Glyphs [FCI05]. They used a combination of parallel coordinates and star glyphs to provide a more efficient analysis compared to the original parallel coordinates.

Pinzger *et al.* with RelVis [PGFL05] use a similar metaphor as the star glyphs to look at the relations within the software entities and their historical changes. They proposed to use the so called Kiviat diagrams to visualize condensed graphical views on source code and relation history data. In their Kiviat diagram, metric values of different releases are reflected like annual rings on a tree-stump. The diagrams can be used to show one metric in multiple modules or multiple metrics in one module. Furthermore relation of modules are characterized with connections between those modules (Figure 2.10).

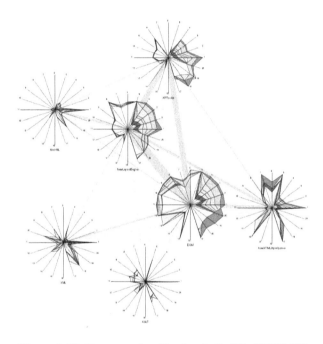

Figure 2.10: Program visualization in RelVis [PGFL05]

Software visualizations can provide a concise overview of a complex software system. Unfortunately, since software has no physical shape, there is no *natural* mapping of software to a two-dimensional space.

In an attempt of using visualizations where position and distance have a meaning. Kuhn *et al.* proposed a consistent layout for software maps in which the position of a software artifact reflects its vocabulary, and distance corresponds to similarity of vocabulary [KLN08]. They used Latent Semantic Indexing (LSI) to map software artifacts to a vector space, and then use Multidimensional Scaling (MDS) to map this vector space down to two dimensions. The results are visualized as software maps with a tool called Software Cartographer (Figure 2.11).

Figure 2.11: Program visualization of an evolving software map [KLN08]

Our visualization approach distinguishes itself from others in that it uses a 3D view to avoiding space limitations. Furthermore we use appropriate layout algorithms combined with intuitive navigation and filtering to prevent dispensable overlapping and grant access to relevant entities details.

2.2 Cognitive Visual Comprehention

Metaphors have been used in poetry and rhetoric all the way back to the ancient greeks. For psychologist's such as Lakoff and Johnson metaphors are an important part of our communication and are used pervasively in human communication [LJ80]. According to Gentner [GG03] cognitive processes underlying metaphor comprehension may reflect the unique nature of human intelligence. And for neuropsychologists such as Schmidt *et al.* [SKCC10] understanding the neural basis of metaphor and the forms of its breakdown is a major goal.

Liu and Kennedy [LK97] worked on form symbolism and the implied analogies. In their work the subjects were asked which word they would match to shapes such as a circle or square. According to them if test persons are asked to match circle and square with warm, cold, weak and strong, they will match the circle with warm and weak and the square with cold and strong.

To use metaphors as a fundamental part of data visualization has been addressed since the seventies. In particular we mention Tufte's work in the mid seventies that emboss the way we present information [TH99]. With his sparklines he presented a simple, condensed way to present trends. He also introduced the terms data-ink ratio and chartjunk, to distinguish useless quantitative data visualization and bring the attention to meaningful visual elements.

Particular work in cognitive comprehension was performed by Chernoff in his work on face distinction and data representation [Che73]. Chernoff mapped multivariate data to the shape of a human face (Figure 2.12). The idea is derived from the ability of humans to recognize faces and notice small changes. Since then other researchers have been working on extending this idea, such as Flury and Riedwyl in [FR81b]. They analyzed the opportunities to use asymmetrical Chernoff faces.

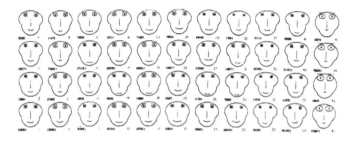

Figure 2.12: Example of various chernoff faces [Che73]

In software visualization the use of metaphors is an important medium to explain the abstract contexts of software projects. Similar to Liu and Kennedy in [LK97]. Often simple forms such as squares, cylinders, and cubes are used. Lanza and Ducasse for example used squares as a basic metaphor for their Polymetric Views [LD03] whereas Loewe and Panas used cubes as a basic metaphor in their work on Vizz3d [LP05].

Within our approach we use metaphors for the glyphs of our software entities. In representing software entities with glyphs, that we know from our daily lives we aim at an improved software comprehension compared to abstract graphical representation.

2.3 Audio

Supporting the understanding of complex data, especially if a software visualization is not able to completely facilitate the understanding of the present situation, opens a new field of interest. We think that audio promises benefits in such situations. Up to the point of our research only little work is present in supporting a software visualization with audio. Work up to now focused more on using audio in the context of software analysis and auditory display.

A good introduction to the various approaches in the area of external auditory representations of programs can be found in Vicker's work [Vic04]. In his summary he gives a brief historical review and addresses the characteristics of the main program auralisation systems.

With the focus on our work, Baecker *et al.* use audio to provide programmers with debugging and profiling feedback without disturbing the integrity of the graphical interface [BDA97]. For them audio is a more salient representation for certain types of program information such as repetitious patterns in control flow and nonlinear sequences of variable values.

For Berman and Gallagher audio offers simple ways for program comprehension activities [BG06]. They present techniques to listen to program slices and help software developers in undertaking such program comprehension activities.

Stefik *et al.* [SAPB07] addressed software analysis with audio. With their Wicked Audio Debugger, they show how to use aural feedback to sonify computer code as an aid to non-sighted programmers. In their feasibility study they show that participants were able to comprehend around 86 percent of dynamic program behavior while only listening to the aural feedback.

Our use of audio is focused more on supporting an user in his interaction within a visualization. While others focus on tracking state variables and control flow during debugging, or visualizing algorithms, we think that combining audio with a software visualization can help an user to find the relevant aspects he is looking for.

2.4 Automated Comprehension Tasks

Automated comprehension tasks in our understanding are a set of preconfigured tasks that help in the creation of a meaningful software visualization for common tasks. Research has been working on what common tasks software engineers and programmers ask regularly. In the following we present some of these exponents.

Letovsky presents a taxonomy of questions programmers ask while performing change tasks [Let98]. In his empirical study he analysed verbal protocols of professional programmers as they were engaged in program comprehension tasks. He classified the different types of cognitive events and derived his model out of programmers mental processes.

Johnson and Erdem studied questions asked to experts on a newsgroup [LA95]. In their empirical studies inquiries of episodes were conducted in order to investigate the kinds of questions users ask, their relation to the user's task and level of expertise. Their results were embodied in a tool called I-Doc.

Erdos and Sneed based their work on personal experience [ES98]. In their opinion it is only necessary to comprehend the sectors affected by the maintenance request in order to maintain a program. As a result of their work they propose seven kinds of questions programmers must answer while performing a change task. The questions address invocation of subroutines, the arguments and answers of a method, control flows, declaration and access of program entities.

Sillito *et al.* worked on figuring out the kind of questions programmers ask when evolving a code base [SMV06]. To achieve that, they observed on two qualitative studies what questions participants asked while performing change tasks to medium and large sized programs. Based on their empirical results they generalized and presented a comprehensive list of 44 common questions.

With our approach we extended those questions based on empirical studies and implemented those solvable with a visualization approach into our workflow. In doing so we aim at a more interactive approach for analyzing a software system and guiding users to identify relevant aspects.

2.5 Multi-Touch Technologies

Multitouch technologies have been around for a long time and a variety of different approaches implement the same principal ideas. Still only today's computational power allowed its use on consumer products such as mobile devices and multitouch tables. In the following we describe some of the earlier presence of these technologies.

One of the first multitouch systems was described with the 'Flexible Machine Interface' by Nimish Mehta in 1982 [Meh82]. It consisted of a glass panel showing a black spot, whose size depended on finger pressure allowing a multitouch input picture drawing with simple image processing.

Around the same time at the Bell Labs, Nakatani and Rohrlich provided a discussion on screen based user interfaces [NR83]. In the paper they outline attributes that make multitouch systems attractive for certain contexts and applications. Their so called 'Soft Machines' consist of displaying computer graphics as 'soft controls' on a touch screen to make soft controls operable like conventional hard controls.

Lee *et al.* presented a prototype of a touch-sensitive tablet that is capable of sensing more than one point of contact at a time [LBS85]. In their work they also discuss how multitouch sensing, interpolation, and degree of contact sensing can be combined to expand the vocabulary of human-computer interaction. In their prototype the touches are scanned with a recursive area subdivision.

Han [Han05] describes a simple, inexpensive, and scalable technique for enabling high-resolution multi-touch sensing. To achieve that he used a technology from biometric and robot sensing known as frustrated total internal reflection (FTIR) and applied the concepts to a rear-projector. The described touch screen offers full imaging touch information without occlusion or ambiguity issues. To capture the touches he applies simple image processing operations such as rectification, background subtraction, noise removal, and connected components analysis on each of the 30 frames per seconds.

With DiamondTouch Dietz and Leigh describe a technique for creating a touch-sensitive input device that allows multiple, simultaneous users to interact in an intuitive fashion [DL01]. With their approach the surface generates location dependent, modulated electric fields which allows determination of touch location independently for each user. With that each touch on a common surface is associated with a particular user.

Rekimoto presented an interactive surface that is sensitive to human hand and finger gestures [Rek02] . The sensor recognized multiple hand positions and their shapes. To calculate the distances between the hands and the surface a mesh-shaped antenna is used. In contrast to camera-based gesture recognition systems this method does not suffer from lighting and occlusion problems.

We are interested in using the principal ideas of the multitouch technologies for the interaction with the visual cognitive software entities. With the use of tactile devices, we aim at offering an interactive approach for analyzing a software system perfectly suitable in a collaborative environment.

2.6 Collaboration in Software Engineering

Collaboration over the years has been addressed by many research communities. For us, it is important to see that the more complex a software project gets, the more important an adequate collaboration environment becomes. In particular we focus on how a group of developers can leverage; for their benefit, a combination of software visualization and collaboration approaches. As exponents of collaboration we mention the research done in the community of online learning environments (OLEs) and of Computer Supported Cooperative Work (CSCW).

Hiltz addresses potential negative social effects of online courses [Hil98]. In this work he shows how online courses need collaborative learning strategies, with relatively small classes or groups actively mentored by an instructor, to be as effective as traditional classroom courses. For him collaborative learning is important to the success of asynchronous learning networks (ALNs).

In the community of Computer Supported Cooperative Work (CSCW) we find a basis in the growing interest of product developers in supporting networked groups. Grudin with his article offers a good historical overview [Gru94] together with a discussion on the differences within America, Europe, and Japan. For him CSCW is a forum bringing together researchers and developers who share some but not all interests and must overcome the difficulties of multidisciplinary interaction.

Closer to the software engineering community we find Whitehead's roadmap [Whi07]. He presented an overview of the goals of collaboration in software engineering together with a brief survey of existing collaboration tools. For him, the focus on model oriented collaboration embedded within a larger process is what distinguishes collaboration research in software engineering from broader collaboration research. Among possible future directions for collaboration in software engineering he sees a tight integration between web and desktop development environments and a broader participation by customers and end users in the entire development process.

Among the oldest and most used collaboration tools, we also have to mention email, calendar, chat, and wikis. Adequately exchanging data between online tools has been part of the semantic web community. The semantic web community in particular aims for a web of data that can be processed by machines. As an exponent for such data exchange, we mention Reif *et al.*'s work done on the Semantic Clipboard [RMG06]. With their work they present ways to transfer data across applications while preserving the semantics of the data.

Our COCOVIZ approach aims at applying useful collaboration concepts to the use cases of software development and maintenance, and adequately combine them with automated software analysis and intuitive visualizations.

2.7 Résumé

With this thesis we find ourselves in a crossover of several technologies and communities. One can certainly ask whether one particular technology is necessary in software engineering or doubt the benefit of some technology. Still, we are convinced that only in combining these technologies we get closer to a natural interaction with virtual data. Advantages can be summarized as follows:

1. *Cognitive perception of virtual entities.* With our approach we can match virtual entities to familiar natural objects. Compared to the state-of-the-art a perception of data is facilitated as the observer already is familiar with the used metaphors. We rely on these metaphors in Chapter 3.

2. *Guided analysis of data.* To analyze a software visualization other approaches often require a second visualization. When using audio on top of a visualization an observer can address the audio to support the visual impression and preserve the focus on the primer software visualization. Our aural approach is presented in Chapter 4.

3. *Intuitive collaboration.* Current visualizations are often not intuitive because controls within the visualization and the capabilities to share information limit an observer's workflow. In a multi-touch environment we can arrange the access to adequate controls in an intuitive and natural way and leverage the multiuser capabilities of tactile devices together with information sharing approaches. Our tactile approach is presented in Chapter 6.

Part II

Approach

3

Visual Approach

The visual approach forms the basis of our interactive software system analysis. The main idea of this approach is to use simple and well-known graphical elements from daily life such as houses or cities. Such elements allow an user to quickly and intuitively understand a given visualization via their proportions and shapes.

We present different such metaphors and show how we configure the software metrics to optimize their graphical representations. Our approach is based on a programming language independent format and offers imports from several file formats. This allows us to use our approach in many software projects.

The remainder of this chapter is structured as follows: In Section 3.1 we explain the basics of our visual approach. Section 3.2 discusses the architecture underneath our COCOVIZ approach. In Section 3.3 we explain how to import datasets into CO-COVIZ. Section 3.4 deals with the interactive ideas behind our visual approach and in Section 3.5 we illustrate the visualization components we have been experimenting with.

3.1 Basics

The visual approach explained in this chapter is a type of metric visualization. Across this thesis we optimize our visual approach for software related concerns. Nevertheless, because of its ability to present data in a metaphoric representation the approach allows an application in other fields and with other datasets. We especially see potential in biology for venom analysis and in economy where banks need to compare several financial products.

3.2 Architecture

The general architecture in COCOVIZ is based on the Model-View-Controller paradigm [Ree79]. The Model and View level are further subclassed to preserve independency from the used third party data and graphic frameworks (Figure 3.1). The most important controllers are the model-, the camera-, the sv-mixer- and the visualization-controllers. The model-controller handles all the queries to the database to gather information about the software entities that need to be displayed. The software visualization mixer-controller (SV-Mixer) is used to configure a visualization according to the dataset, the available software-metrics and the user's needs. The camera-controller handles all user interactions and updates to the visualization. The visualization-controller combines all the information and updates the View.

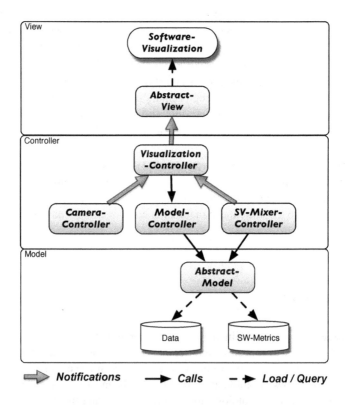

Figure 3.1: The MVC-architecture of COCOVIZ

3.2.1 Data-Model

To assure that our data-model can store language independent source code information, we based the relevant parts on the Famix data format. Famix is a language independent meta-model which was developed in the FAMOOS project [DTP99]. Its purpose is to describe the static structure of object-oriented software systems. The smallest defined entity is a FamixObject. A FamixObject has a reference to a source code object and it allows to add a comment. The most common FamixObjects are subclasses of FamixEntity. They have at least a unique-name and an inheritance structure. Common representations are FamixClass, FamixPackage, FamixMethod and FamixAttribute. The other common FamixObjects are FamixAssociations defining a relation between two FamixObjects. Common representations are FamixInvocation, FamixInheritanceDefinition and FamixAccess.

Apart from Famix-related entities, our data-model defines other visualization and information specific components: Report-, developer-, visual-, metric- and metric-analyse-objects. Visual-object holds visual information about a FamixObject such as shape, color, and used layout algorithm. In a metric-analyse-object we store one particular metric measurement distinguished by a FamixObject, its version, and a metric. Report-objects store information about a FamixEntity's Bug- or Modificationreport and developer-objects store information related to the developer.

3.3 Creation of dataset

As discussed before, COCOVIZ uses a data model based on Famix. To import data into the application we developed an extensible importer and provided a variety of acceptable data formats. In the following we explain the accepted file formats.

3.3.1 Evolizer

The Evolizer project[1] is a suite of Eclipse plug-ins developed at the S.E.A.L. Group of the University of Zurich. It allows one to parse and analyze software repositories. Evolizer stores the data in a so called Release History Data Base (RHDB) as explained in [FPG03].

---

[1]http://www.evolizer.org, last checked 14.1.2012

3.3.2 Together

Together is a commercial suite of tools[2] built on top of eclipse that among other things allows one to calculate a variety of metrics on a project and to export them in an XML file format.

3.3.3 Eclipse Metrics Plugin

The metrics plug-in for eclipse is an open source project[3] dedicated to calculate a set of metrics from any eclipse project. It offers an export functionality into an own file format, that COCOVIZ is able to read.

3.3.4 MSE

The MSE file-format is a generic file format used for import-export in Moose. Moose is a platform for software and data analysis[4]. MSE is a generic file format that can describe any other data model. It is a meta-format similar to the XML standard[5].

3.4 Filtering

One of the key ideas behind our visual approach, is to adapt the visualization to the current needs of a software engineer. An engineer should be capable of eliminating the entities that are not of current interest and that are not relevant for a particular discussion.

We call our implementation for this architecture Software Visualization Mixer (SV-Mixer). Similar to an audio mixer used in professional recording studios, our SV-Mixer has multiple channels consisting of a slider with filters, that are easily adjusted. Every channel represents a connection from a metric or data representation to what we call a visual representation (*e.g.*. the x-coordinate of a visualized entity). Moving the channel slider adjusts the attached filter values and notifies the visualization controller to update (Figure 3.1). To help an engineer to apply such filters, every mixer-channel shows the distribution of the attached metric among the dataset in a graphical representation (Figure 3.2). The graphical representation has

---

[2]http://www.borland.com/us/products/together/index.html, last checked 14.1.2012
[3]http://metrics.sourceforge.net, last checked 14.1.2012
[4]http://www.moosetechnology.org last checked 14.1.2012
[5]http://www.w3.org last checked 14.1.2012

two graphs: the green graph shows the distribution of the metric among the visualized entities and the blue graph shows the distribution accross all entities in the dataset.

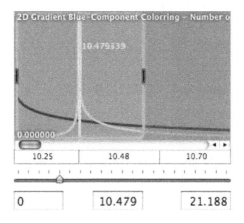

Figure 3.2: SV-Mixer's graphical representation of a metrics distribution

3.5 Visualization

The visualization consists of a set of entities, their shape and their attached layout, color, and textures algorithms. The ideal type of applied algorithms varies from case to case.

3.5.1 Mapping

Every algorithm registers a number of channels for the needed visual representations with the SV-Mixer (Figure 3.3). As explained previously, in the SV-Mixer visual representations are mapped to a metric or data representation. For example, a layout algorithm that takes two input metrics to calculate the x and y values registers two channels with the SV-Mixer. A color algorithm that takes one metric to color, color the entities, registers only one channel.

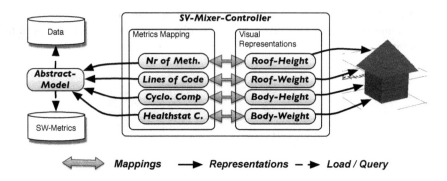

Figure 3.3: Mapping metrics to visual representation

3.5.2 Metaphors and Glyphs

Glyphs are objects visualized from a set of software metrics. Similar to the algorithms a glyph registers the number of needed channels with the SV-Mixer. The mapped metrics value is then used to calculate specific glyphs for a software entity (Figure 3.3). Within COCOVIZ we introduce glyphs representing a metaphor, which attempts to visualize a software in a comprehensible way. The goal is to contribute to a faster cognition of the relevant aspects in visualization compared to glyphs without a metaphor (*e. g.* Starglyphs [FCI05]). A viewer can thus quickly distinguish a well-shaped glyph from a miss-shaped one, or categorizes entities just by their shape. If beyond that the metrics are normalized accurately the resulting visualization intuitively provides orientation about good-designed aspect in the represented software and distressed ones. In the following, we explain three metaphors in further detail: the house metaphor, the table metaphor, and the spear metaphor.

House Metaphor. The idea is to represent software entities as houses. With normalized metrics a well-designed class will then look like a well-shaped house, whereas a problematic class resembles a miss-shaped house (Figure 3.4). To build a simple house of this metaphor, we use four parameters (visual representations) together with their metric mappings. Two metrics represent the width and height of the roof, the other two metrics represent the width and height of the house body (Figure 3.3). In Figure 3.4 we mapped the two roof parameters to size metrics and the body parameters to complexity metrics (Figure 3.6 a). If we look at the house in Figure 3.4 a) we see a complex class, represented by a large body (cube). The large roof of the house on the other side suggests that the class has as well a reasonable size. If we compare the house with the one in Figure 3.4 b) we see that the second one shows a similar roof size as the left house. The represented class therefore has to have a notable size, too. However, the house body is notably smaller than its roof. The house metaphor suggests that we have to pay further attention to this class. Still, a miss-shaped house does not conclude that there is something wrong with the represented entity. It just shows an uncommon state in the visualized context. In Figure 3.4 b) a similar class could result as well from a design decision to implement a data-class. The same way a well-shaped house as in Figure 3.4 a) does not mean that we do not have to care about such an entity at all. The shown house for example has a notable size compared to the other entities in the same context as seen in Figure 3.4. In such a situation even if the house looks well-shaped the general size suggests that the entity is considered a problematic candidate to maintain and evolve, a potential GodClass as explained by Lanza and Marinescu in [LM06].

We investigated practicability of visualizations with the house metaphor within 2 and 3 dimensions. In the 2D visualization, the roof is drawn as a triangle with metric values for its width and height and the body of the house as a rectangle with two further metric values for its width and height. In both cases problematic classes result in a variety of miss-shaped glyphs.

Interestingly, in both dimensions some miss-shaped houses resembles other familiar metaphors such as a conifer or fir tree or a church tower. In normalizing the metrics adequately these special cases of miss-shaped houses represent special categories of classes and are easily perceived throughout the visualization.

Figure 3.4: Glyphs of a house metaphor: a) well-shaped b) miss-shaped house

Table Metaphor. The table metaphor is based on the idea to represent software entities as tables. A well-designed class looks like a well-leveled table, whereas, a problematic class results in a non-planar table. To build a table metaphor, we use four parameters (visual representations) and their metric mappings; each of the met-

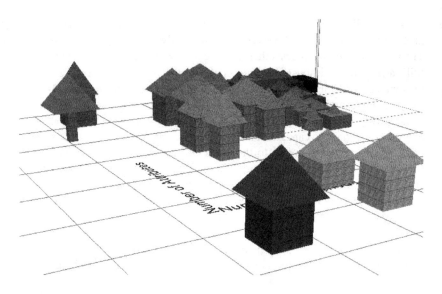

Figure 3.5: A visualization using house metaphor

rics is mapped to a table-leg (Figure 3.6 b). The table-legs are represented as four cylinders with a rectangle as tabletop placed above the legs. The mapped metrics are normalized to the size of an ideal table leg. A well-designed class with adequately normalized metrics is than perceived as a well-shaped table. Problematic classes are perceived as tabletops bevelled to the right, left, front, or back. The table metaphor offers an interesting way to perceive strange software components with a simple metahpor-based glyph showing even or leaning tables. Experimenting with the table metaphor in a similar way as with the house metaphor revealed that the table metaphor was less effective than the house metaphor. A number of factors are suggested to explain this difference in effectiveness: the same cohesion is not as easily visible in the table metaphor as compared to the house metaphor. Even though the metrics are simply mapped to the table legs, the table metaphor is more complex to understand for the viewer because of the tables' symmetries when navigating around the system in a 3D visualization. It quickly becomes difficult to preserve which metric represents which leg. However, well-formed and miss-formed tables can easily be spotted with the table metaphor. The table metaphor offers a good and intuitive overview to find candidates for design anomalies. We see use for this metaphor in situations where metrics values are discrete or a basic distinction is enough to tag candidates before addressing them in other more perceivable views.

Spear Metaphor. In the spears metaphor a well-designed software entity looks like a well-formed spear. To build this metaphor, we use three parameters (visual representations) in combination with their metric mappings for the spear shaft's width and height and to its spike height (Figure 3.6 c). The spear shaft is represented as a cylinder with two spikes represented as cones on both ends of the shaft. A miss-shaped glyph thus looks like a very long or a very wide spear. Beyond that representation additional metrics can be mapped on the spear stripes. The spear metaphor is similar to the house metaphor in that 3D navigation does not impede understanding the visualization. However, the metaphor does not resemble any other well-known objects such as the fire-tree in the house-metaphor, that would allow to additionally categorize problematic classes. In Figure 3.6 c) the height of a spear is mapped to the *number of functions*, the width to the *lines of code* and the spear point represents the *Cyclomatic Complexity* metric.

In a visualization using the spear metaphor special attention is granted to all small fat spears that are visible, as they represent large classes with few functions. A notably sized spear top suggests that the entity may be problematic to maintain and evolve. A benefit for the spear metaphor is that we can map *fan in* and bug metrics to the stripes. If a problematic candidate beside being large and complex also feature many *bug reports* and many *incoming accesses* (orange to red strips) that than emphasize the candidate as an already problematic and critical components.

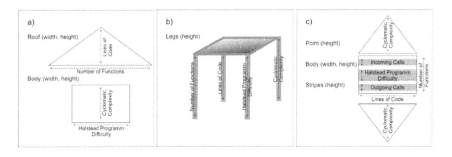

Figure 3.6: Mapping of a) House- b) Table- c) Spear-Metaphors

3.5.3 Layouts

Where multiple entities are visualized it becomes essential to layout them adequately. In software visualization, we often start with thousands of software entities, before applying context specific filters. Some of the basic layout algorithms such as arrangements in circles or chessboard, just prevent the thousands of glyphs from overlapping or hiding relevant aspects and sustain the overall comprehensibility. At the Università della Svizzera Italiana, Richard Wettel and Michele Lanza experiment with similar layout algorithms that offer a better observation of the glyphs in a visualization of large sets of software entities [WL07].

In our approach layouts cover an even more essential part of our approach, if we consider them as an part of the interaction. For example, a layout algorithm can use parameters (visual representations) to calculate an entity's position based on its metrics. In such a layout the overlapping becomes secondary. The focus is suddenly more in using a layout adapted to a use case to support an engineer in a fast perception of relevant aspects. Fischer *et al.* [FPG03] and Kuhn *et al.* [KLN08] presented such approaches in using a force directed-layout algorithm to layout entities based on their relation among each other.

The primary goal of a layout thus is to adequately present a specific set of glyphs based on the dataset.

3.5.4 2D and 3D

In our approach, the third dimension is used for general navigation, filtering and selection, before flipping to a detailed representation in a two-dimensional view. We do so because a three-dimensional navigation space has the benefit of dipping into the visualization in a horizontal or vertical view. Software structures can be perceived on a voyage in a virtual world. Nevertheless, a third dimensional view has the drawback that too much information and overlapping glyphs can menace to spot relevant aspects. As the metric mapping for the third dimension is not always beneficial, we switch to a two-dimensional visualization where proportions and relevant aspects can be illustrated in a more cognitive way. Such a combination allows an adequate combination of both dimensions.

3.5.5 Tagging Glyphs and Visualization States

In CocoViz we implemented a concept to preserve visualization states or remember interesting glyphs for later analysis. We do so since during the navigation within a visualization, relevant aspects are spotted and need to be remembered before proceeding with the interaction. The remembered aspects can then be analyzed later or shared within the work group. To dynamically interact in a three-dimensional view such a functionality becomes far more important as it allows one to mark the interacting trail and prevents from getting lost within the visualization. Furthermore such a functionality allows switching to other visualizations and examining the spotted aspects from another view. Our approach offers two interoperability modes for this issue.

- We offer one to tag an interesting element while navigating through a view. With this interoperability specific elements can be remembered for later analysis or visualization in another view.

- We can save the actual view as a snapshot. A snapshot is then used to go back to a certain state or to share spotted aspects within the working group.

3.6 Case Study

For the case study we used a data set of the Mozilla project [6]. In particular, we used the same data set used in the projects by Pinzger *et al.* [PGFL05] and Fischer *et al.* [FPG03]. The data set contains the full Mozilla program code with around 1.7 million lines of code and evolutionary data of seven releases from version 0.92 to version 1.7. The metrics were calculated per release.

Across the dissertation, we mainly use the house metaphor as an adequate visual representation. In this first simple use case, we had a look onto the Mozilla project, using the spear metaphor. We started our inspection with a visualization that maps size-complexity-metrics to the objects (System Hot-Spot-View). This view shows us complex software components that condense a variety of functionality. As stated before such components are difficult to maintain and evolve and are candidates for design anomalies such as God Classes. Figure 3.7 on the left shows an overview of version 1.7.

At first glance we note two extreme types of spears. The small long and the fat large spears. The small long spears represent classes which have many functions but are small in size. An example would be *nsHTMLTableCellElement* (Figure 3.7a) , which is a part of the complex Document Object Model (DOM)-Module. The class is used to represent HTML content and has 96 functions on 552 lines of code. Classes from that type might as well be more complex (*e. g.* if they implement an algorithm). They could have many bugs or be critical parts of the application as a central and widely used element. However, they turn out to be simple classes such

---

[6]http://www.mozilla.org last checked 14.1.2012

as interface declarations. To ensure that our classes are less critical, we us the SV-Mixer to temporary filter out the classes that are less complex. We filter out classes that have very few reported bugs and few incoming access calls.

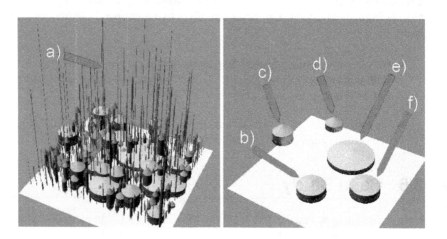

Figure 3.7: Spear Metaphor showing a System Hot-Spot-View of Mozilla: the left shows an overview; from where on the right side potential candidates were sequentially filtered out.

The second extreme type of classes, represented as large fat spears, has a notable amount of functions and is large in size. These candidates are considered more problematic to maintain and evolve. To see the potential candidates we filter the classes based on their lines of code and hide the smallest 30%. We further want to know which of these are complex and therefore critical. This information can be retrieved by applying a filter based on a complexity metric. We also argue that incoming data calls are more important, as they represent how the classes are used in the system, and therefore filter on an incoming data call metric. Therewith, we reduce the classes to five critical candidates. To verify whether those candidates really are critical for the Mozilla project, we take a closer look at our metrics and the information provided by the official Mozilla developer site[7].

The *nsGlobalWindow* (Figure 3.7c) as the previously mentioned *nsHTMLTableCel-lElement* is part of the complex Document Object Model (DOM)-Module. The class is used to open windows with the represented HTML content and its interaction. It

---

[7]http://www.mozilla.org/owners.html last checked 14.1.2012

has 230 functions in 6193 lines of code. It accesses 36 functions from other classes and its functions are used by 7 functions from other modules. We further note that it has over 100 non trivial problem reports. *nsGlobalWindow* thus clearly can be regarded as a design critical component.

nsSelection (Figure 3.7b) and *nsCSSParser* (Figure 3.7d) are found within the DOM-Content-Module and are used to interact with selections and the parsing CSS files. These classes have 211 functions in 7749 lines of code and 112 functions in 5530 lines of code, they are obviously not small either. Both have over 40 and 20 non trivial problem-reports respectively *nsSelection* might be less critical as it does not provide basic functionality and is accessed only from one other class.

The *nsPresShell* (Figure 3.7f) is found in the layout engine HTML-module, which Mozilla uses for rendering tree construction, layouts, images, etc. The presentation shell (*nsPresShell*) is used for arena allocations and response to user or script actions like window resizing, document's default font changes or drag & drop operations. It has 226 functions in 8013 lines of code. It uses 242 functions from other classes and its functions are accessed by 7 functions from other modules. In addition, it comprises more than 130 non trivial problem-reports. Clearly *nsPresShell* is a central and design critical component, too.

Last but not least *nsCSSFrameConstructor* within the same HTML-Module handles CSS Frames (Figure 3.7e). It has 210 functions in 13494 lines of code. It uses 813 functions from other classes and is accessed by 10 functions from other modules. With over 200 non trivial problem-reports it is obviously at least as design critical as the previously mentioned classes.

Within our quick tour through the case study, we still have not focused on many details yet, but we have easily filtered hotspots. Further options are 1) tagging the elements of our interest and further analyzing them in other visualizations; 2) inspect whether there were surprisingly many changes to particular classes over the last revisions; and 3) compare the tagged elements by applying other metric-cluster. Nevertheless we showed that with few simple steps we can focus on the essential parts of a system.

3.7 Résumé

With our visual approach we are able to use the cognitive knowledge of an observer to improve his perception. An adequate mapping of software characteristics to objects known from daily life assists an observer to distinguish relevant aspects from less relevant ones. Software components with this approach become easily distinguishable and comparable trough their visual representation. A further benefit of this approach is that the use of known objects allows us to involve people such as software engineers, project leaders, and managers not completely familiar with the details of the visualized software components in a general discussion. We present the validation in Part III.

4

Aural Approach

The aural approach is intended to work hand in hand with our visual approach. The visual approach allows one to simplify software visualization and facilitate cognitive perception through adequate layouting and filtering. In situations where layouting and filtering is not enough and results still show hundreds of software entities, other solutions must be considered. In our work it is suggested that these situations can be addressed using additional information: audio. The main idea of using audio is to grant simple access to hidden information and acoustically guiding an observer towards relevant aspects of his analysis.

We present two main approaches for supporting software visualization with audio (entity and ambient audio) and show how to use them in combination with the underlying software metrics and graphical representations.

The remainder of this chapter is structured as follows: In Section 4.1 we explain the basics of our aural approach. Section 4.2 shows how we structured audio support in COCOVIZ. In Section 4.3 we explain how to use audio to gather information of one particular entity. Section 4.4 presents how to use audio to notify and guide an observer towards particular entities.

4.1 Basics

The aural approach explained in this chapter is built in conjunction with the previously explained cognitive glyphs. However, the generation of aural feedback is not dependent on the cognitive glyph approach and can be used combined with other visualizations.

The main limitation we found in our aural approach resides in an adequate generation of the aural feedback. During our work we experimented with the abilities to generate aural feedback in various representations. In this thesis, we address the use of tonal-synthesized tunes, feedback generated with a speak synthesizer, alteration of audio samples, and 3D-audio positioning.

4.2 Architecture

To support audio within COCOVIZ, we extended the architecture with a dedicated audio-controller that handles the change notifications and notifies the adequate algorithms when recalculations to the audio-representation are needed (Figure 4.1). The audio-controllers similar to the visualization-controllers registers for change notifications with the model, the camera and the SV-Mixer-controllers. On top of that the visualization-controller notifies relevant changes resulting from a layout algorithm.

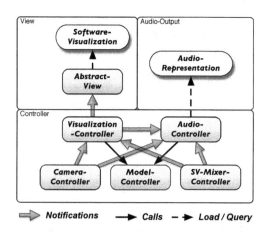

Figure 4.1: The MVC-architecture of COCOVIZ with audio support

4.3 Entity Audio

Entity Audio is intended as an aural feedback representing the characteristics of one particular software entity. An explanation shall illustrate the usefulness of this approach.

We already mentioned that during software visualization situations arise where with all the layout and filtering an observer finds himself among hundreds of entities.

To continue an analysis an observer in a traditional visual approach often ends up creating another visualization. Such sub-visualisations, however, can distract an observer from his main task. To overcome these shortcomings of visualizations we looked at components that are fundamental to simplify the program understanding and navigation.

According to Pennington's bottom-up theory of program comprehension a programmer focuses first on the basic structural entities [Pen87a,Pen87b]. We therefore have to consider an adequate highlighting of basic text structure units as a fundamental component.

Mosemann and Wiedenbeck, on the other hand, addressed the navigation performance and stated that reading a program by following the control flow offers an ideal way for comprehension even for novices [MW01] .

Pacione proposed ways to increase the utility of visualization for software comprehension [Pac04]. According to him a visualization can be classified into five levels of abstraction for software comprehension. He suggested that software comprehension is facilitated if we can adequately use multiple of those levels of abstraction combined with multiple facets and the integration of static and dynamic information.

Pacione *et al.* also performed case studies in a realistic software comprehension scenario [PRW03]. According to their results, visualizing an object- or class-level representation of the system and providing an architectural-level view are optimal in terms of answering most of the scenario questions.

From Pacione's perspective, our cognitive software visualization approach can be placed in between the object-/class- representation and architectural-level. To enhance our approach and adequately use multiple of the levels suggested by Pacione we looked at concepts such as pop-ups and audio.

Popups or tooltips allow an observer to access additional information on entities in a little box. Such popups are commonly used in other visualization tools. Implementing these concepts for our purpose showed a number of problems: (1) showing a tooltip instantly results in having a disturbing box on top of our visualization; (2) with more than ten entities to investigate, tooltips become suboptimal, showing too much information and eventually ending up distracting the observer from the main task.

Supporting our visualization with audio, prevents us from having to present all the details of additional information. Instead, just enough feedback can be given to allow further classification of an entity. In this manner, the previously mentioned shortcomings in relation to tooltips can also be avoided.

4.3.1 Mapping

To create aural feedback similar to the visual approach an algorithm registers a number of channels for the needed variables with the SV-Mixer. (Figure 4.2) These representations are again mapped to a metric or data representation. For example, our evolutionary audio algorithm needs two input metrics to calculate the changes from the previous entity.

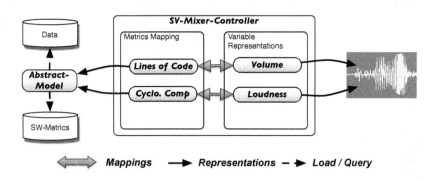

Figure 4.2: Mapping metrics to audio representation

4.3.2 Detect exceeding thresholds

One of the simplest aural feedbacks is to notify an observer if a mapped metric with extended information is exceeding a threshold. When the observer clicks on the entity, the algorithm checks whether an entity exhibits a metric value beyond a specified value. If this is the case a sound or simple acoustic signal is played. Such an approach is particularly convenient in cases where the observer is looking for entities that are outliers in any particular metric. For instance, in a software visualization, we are interested in entities for which many critical bugs are reported. An audio annotation showing exceeding threshold is used to map *Nr of critical Bugs* to the entities and get notified which entities in the visualization have more than the specified number of critical bugs.

A slightly modified version of the simple threshold algorithm, allows one to track not only threshold exceedings but also intervals. The advantage of intervals is, that now an observer can check with an audio feedback to which subgroup an entity would belong in an extended or completely different context from the currently visualized one. Imagine to map *JUnit test Coverage* to entities and classify how well particular critical entities have been tested.

4.3.3 Detect design anomalies

The detecting of design anomalies has similarities to the previous idea. The difference is that it runs a short analysis on an entity before giving a feedback. Consider a situation where we would like to know if an entity is affected by a particular design anomaly. Design anomalies are often refereed to as code smells or anti-patterns in source code. Different approaches exist to detect such patterns, in our work, we build on the pattern detection described in *Metrics in Practice* by Lanza and Marinescu [LM06].

A user is determined to select a design anomaly type he wants to check software entities for. Afterwards, he can click on entities and gets notified about the analysis results. In a traditional visual approach, this would probably happen again in a pop-up or by coloring the detected entities according to a color concept. In an audio-supported visualization, an entity can give us a more precise audio feedback. The feedback could be spoken or non-spoken, depending on the need. For instance testing an entity for a set of design anomalies would then speak the result like *'the current entity is a potential god class and a potential shot gun surgery class'*. Of course, spoken text is only a rather simple example of audio support. Harmonies, disharmonies, twang or shrillness are other possibilities to enrich an audio-supported visualization. In summary, compared to the visual only approach, we can get a more informative description of the entity's extended context, including the cases where entities incorporate two or more code smells.

4.3.4 Entity description with synthesized audio

A more sophisticated approach to enrich an entity's feedback with audio is to synthesize the audio feedback based on the related entity's values. Important for this approach is the preservation of the distinction of audio feedback from similar entities. But which sound components allow preservation of this distinction? A lot of research has been done in the field of psycho-acoustics to address the issue of distinguishability. Most of the work is motivated in the context of audio compression. Particularly interesting for our context are the so called *'Zwicker parameters'* [ZFH01]. According to Zwicker *et al.* changes to the parameters *loudness, sharpness, tone pitch, roughness* and *oscillation* do preserve the distinguishability of synthesized audio.

This information allows the generation of highly complex synthesized audio feedback that still remains compact. A simple implementation of such an algorithm can be achieved if we map an entity's metrics to the various Zwicker parameters.

Example 1: A large and long-lived entity with few critical bugs and low coupling. As an example, we map the values for *FanIn* to loudness, the *Number of critical Bugs* to roughness, the *Evolutionary growth rate* to the tone pitch and the *Lines of Code* to the length of the tone. This mapping allows one to perceive a large entity with few critical bugs, that is not used often by other classes and has been in the system for quite some time, most likely as an audio feedback of a *long, clear, but rather low tone.*

Example 2: A large but young entity with many critical bugs and high coupling. With the same mapping explained in Example 1 such an entity, introduced only in recent releases and widely used by other classes with several critical bugs would most likely result in *a long, rough, shrill and loud tone.*
We see advantages for these kinds of mapping in that it allows a generation of an entity's aural footprint based on extended information. Table 4.1 shows two possible mappings of metrics to the Zwicker parameters. We call a set of metrics that together allow one to adequately answer a particular software visualization question a Metric Cluster.

Zwicker Parameter	Structural Metric Cluster	Evolution Metric Cluster
Loudness	Complexity	Fan in
Tone pitch	Growth rate	Growth rate
Roughness	-	# critical Bugs
Oscillation	-	Change rate
Tone length	Lines of Code	Lines of Code

Table 4.1: Example of two metric clusters mapped to synthesized audio concepts

4.3.5 Audio in Evolutionary Analysis

Let us consider how we perceive the changes that occurred to an entity from one release to another in a traditional visualization. Whenever we change the focus of a dataset from one release to another, we usually encounter a variety of simultaneous changes. This can result in the change of positions, disappearance or shrinking in size of objects. It can be difficult to keep track of a particular set of interesting entities during such changes. We can animate the entity changes in position and size, nevertheless with a variety of simultaneous changes, it remains difficult to perceive whether an entity of interest changed substantially from one version to another. Aural feedback allows one to address this in supporting a visualization by simply notifying, whenever an entity of interest changes more than *e. g.* 10% from its previous version. Audio feedback can be spoken or non-spoken, depending on personal preference. For example, the evolutionary change of entities from one version to another can be perceived with a simple spoken annotation such as *'from version 1.0 to 2.0 the tagged entities ListProducer and PersistentModel changed by more than 10 percent.'*

4.3.6   Audio in Trace Analysis

Trace analysis is useful to dynamically test programs components within their use cases. Therefore it has been widely discussed in the program comprehension research community. As part of the Evospaces project[1] Dugerdil and Sazzadul found visual tracing to be an informative way to analyze use cases [DA08]. The bottle-neck of visual tracing resides in the endless amount of visualized actions one can get lost in. Just imagine what actions are called in an iteration. If we visualize the trace as it is, we see how the entity gets called in every iteration. If the focus is on performance issues, this can show us interesting behaviors. However, if our interest is more on what entities get called, a separate visualization of the while-iterations is not necessary. It becomes clear that for trace visualization we need to decide at first what we are looking for, and adequately hide irrelevant information.

Aural feedback, can overcome parts of such downsides differently. We suggest to support visual tracing with audio similar to the one used by Baecker *et al.* to provide programmers with debugging feedback [BDA97]. In our understanding, before visualizing a trace, the entities of interest should be tagged. Visualizing a trace notifies us about interactions that engage our particular set of entities. Even during visualization of system interactions, relevant entities can be tracked.

4.3.7   Case Study

In this case study we present example scenarios while we analyze a software project. We show situations where audio feedback is particularly useful and compare it to the effort that is necessary to achieve the same result with a non audio supported visualization. The used evolutionary data set consists of a exemplar commercial web application framework used in healthcare. We analyzed six releases over the period of 3 years. The metrics were calculated per release. The framework has more than 950 classes and approximately 90'000 lines of code. In the following, we perceive the framework from a program comprehension and a software analysis point of view.

---

[1]http://www.inf.usi.ch/projects/evospaces last checked 14.1.2012

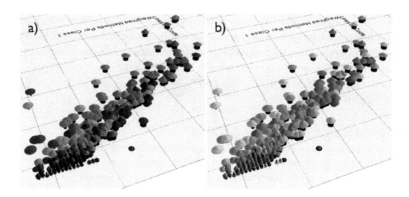

Figure 4.3: House glyphs showing a System Hot-Spot-View of a commercial web application framework in the latest release; in a) colors represent how often the entities use methods from other entities, in b) colors represent the inheritance level of the entities

4.3.8 Program comprehension scenario

In this program comprehension scenario a quality assurance team asks for critical classes of the system. These classes where changed since the last release and need to undergo extensive testing. A set of such critical classes can be found by looking at potential big and complex classes, that are widely used by other classes and have been changed during the last release.

To achieve this, we visualize all the class entities of the application using our house glyphs. The visual representations of the house glyphs are mapped to a Hot-Spot-View (size-complexity-metrics). Such a mapping shows complex software components that condense a variety of functionality. We then arrange the entities on the visualization axes using their *lines of code* and *weighted methods per class* values. The colors in Figure 4.3 a) represent *fanOut*, a metric showing how extensively the classes use other classes. We mapped and configured the different colors in the SV-Mixer to cluster the entities in a sensible way. Classes using methods from less than 4 other classes are colored in blue. Classes that use up to 8 other classes are colored in orange and classes with more than 8 are shown in red.

Figure 4.3 a) shows the classes of our visualization setup. In the upper right corner we see houses that are complex (body size) and large (roof size). In our context of finding crucial system components, we need to take those into account for an in-depth analysis. However, we need to pay attention to some of the smaller classes too, because they might only be small based on their inheritance relationships. To gain confidence on the small but relevant classes, with the current visualization approaches, we need to create a second view. In our scenario, we either do this by changing the layout mapping to rearrange the entities based on their inheritance, or as shown in Figure 4.3 b), by changing the mapping of the colors. In the first case we are confronted with the disadvantage of losing orientation and finding all the entities on a new position, in the second case we at least preserve a comparability between the two views. In any case we lose the focus from our main context, and end up having a less important extra view, making the comprehension of a project as a whole more difficult.

Audio feedback, in our context can address the small crucial classes without losing focus on the primary view. For instance, we can map the *inheritance level* of the entities to give us an audio feedback based on a threshold exceeding audio algorithm. We then hover with the mouse over the entities of our interest and get an audio feedback. Whenever there is an entity that needs further consideration, we can select that entity right away.

With an evolutionary audio algorithm we get an audio feedback on which of these classes were changed during the last release and need extensive testing. The evolutionary audio algorithm notifies changes from the last release with two musical notes playing a interval representing the amount of the change.

To emphasize the usability of audio-supported software visualization for program comprehension, we extend our current example to another common use case. Let us suppose that we are trying to find a bug that was introduced during the latest release. We change focus from our entities of interest to the ones changed during the last release. In a traditional visualization approach, we change the visualization again by mapping the color to the entities changed during the last release. Still, we do not know whether any of the entities under investigation has been changed at all. We have to change focus in our view to gain little or not much information.

Audio support allows us to run our entities through an audio algorithm that notifies us whether the entities were changed during the latest release. We then hover again over the entities under investigation and select the changed ones. We can then analyze these entities in-depth and assure they are not involved with the bug without losing focus.

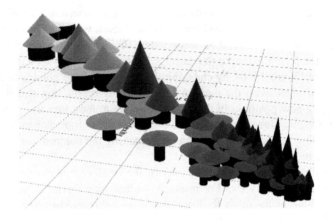

Figure 4.4: House glyphs showing a part of a commercial web application framework in a system hot-spot-view; the brighter the color the higher the god classes potential of a class

4.3.9 Software analysis scenario

A common software analysis scenario is to detect code smells. In a traditional CO-COVIZ approach, we analyze the entities color by a god classes detection algorithm. As shown in Figure 4.4 the brighter the color the higher the god class potential of a class.

If we are further interested in what other code smells the potential god classes are affected, in a visual only approach we can map the color of the entities to another code smell algorithm. With an audio-supported approach, we can run a code smell audio algorithm and hover over the entities under investigation. Without losing focus, we immediately hear what other code smells the potential god classes are potentially affected.

4.4 Ambient Audio

In comparison to entity audio, where we represent characteristics of a software entity, with ambient audio we intend to guide an observer towards what he is currently looking for within the software visualization. Let us consider again a situation where with all the layout and filtering an observer finds himself among hundreds of entities. Entity audio shows a solution to overcome these shortcomings of visualizations. Still, it is suboptimal if an observer has to click on more than ten entities and listen to multiple audio notifications one after the other. Therefore, we looked for a better solution for such a situation with multiple entities. Our goal is to extend the audio support to a more explorative modality. We eliminate the need to click on multiple entities and help an observer in his exploration, by conciliating him through adequate audio sources and guiding him in finding relevant aspects. A first improvement and less time consuming would it be if we were able to play multiple aural feedbacks at the same time and still preserve the distinction among the entities. To enforce that, we looked for cognitive meaningful sound samples that remind us on familiar situation from our daily life. With such samples we can support perception when playing multiple aural feedbacks at a time.

In the following sections, we explain the principle ideas of ambient audio and discuss potential non trivial use cases that benefit from ambient audio.

4.4.1 Mapping

The metric mapping for ambient audio is similar to the one used for the entity audio approach. An algorithm registers a number of channels for the needed variables with the SV-Mixer (Figure 4.2). However, because we overlap multiple aural feedbacks, during our studies we limited the mapping on most algorithms to volume and frequency of a sound sample.

4.4.2 Ambient Audio Software Exploration (AASE)

Ambient Audio Software Exploration uses audio to find a particular entity. Like in a movie or computer game, where the audio track warns the audience / player of upcoming plots. Imagine a thriller movie were a strident ambient sounds warns us of a just arriving event. Similar to the sound of such a thriller we create similar ambient like sounds out of sets of software entities with particular dependencies or relationships.

The ambient sounds are either constructed with the same concepts used for entity audio (selection of classes, filtering, metric clusters, ...) or in mapping the calculations to adequate Zwicker parameters [ZFH01] (frequency / volume) of a particular meaningful sounds sample *e. g.* a bubble sound.

Table 4.2 shows a set of possible case scenarios where ambient audio can be used together with possible mapping criteria.

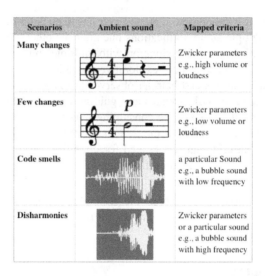

Scenarios	Ambient sound	Mapped criteria
Many changes		Zwicker parameters e.g., high volume or loudness
Few changes		Zwicker parameters e.g., low volume or loudness
Code smells		a particular Sound e.g., a bubble sound with low frequency
Disharmonies		Zwicker parameters or a particular sound e.g., a bubble sound with high frequency

Table 4.2: Scenarios and possible mappings for ambient audio

4.4.3 Triggering AASE

We integrated several ways to trigger an ambient audio source. This allows an observer to choose the preferred one based on his current situation. An observer can ask for an ambient audio with a key combination, with the shift key together with a mouse click, and with a four finger touch on a multitouch table. For complicated 3D visualization situations, we provide access to a head-up display similar to the ones known from video-games (Figure 4.5). Whenever we trigger an AASE an exploration marker becomes visible, that personifies an observer's navigation in the visualization space and pictures the position of the observer's ears. The observer can then move the marker around the visualization (Figure 4.5). While moving the marker around we take its current position and use surround sound techniques to clarify which audio representation is currently played and then adapt the aural notification to the new situation.

For example, let us use AASE with a bubble sound sample. When we move the exploration marker towards a relatively unproblematic area of the analyzed software we would hear an ambient sound similar to a soft sea. When approaching a more problematic area we would perceive a more stormy ambient sound, and close to a critical area the ambient sound resembles the one of boiling water. An observer perceives the new audio sources and can adequately adjust his navigation in the visualization In moving towards boiling water and further away from silent areas. When moving the exploration marker, the audio feedback is constantly adapting to the situation of the new position. An observer acting to these changes can be guided on a trail. Throughout our work, we call this trail an audio exploration path (AEP). The observer can preserve an audit trail with keyframes of his followed AEP, allowing an eventual backtracking to interesting exploration positions.

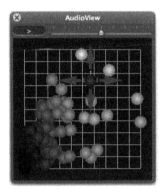

Figure 4.5: Head-up display with exploration marker

4.4.4 Using AASE

The AASE approach enables us to extend the audio support for software visualizations. AASE offers a more explorative modality for an assisted navigation, a space annotated with sounds (AEP) and the perception of dependent entities. Still, we need to discuss when to consider the use of AASE. Ambient audio becomes interesting when the entity characteristics we map to an aural notification representing discrete data. For example when an observer is interested in the present code smells of one entity compared to other entities. Furthermore, the use of AASE can be particularly beneficial if applied in combination with a visualization of dependencies among entities.

Imagine a case scenario where sets of entities are depicted and attention is brought to an entity set with some sort of cohesion among each other (*e. g.* change couplings [GHJ98], number of bug reports). Suppose we are looking for certain instabilities in our system or critically affected system components. We can then build our visualization with a layout involving similarities as used by Fischer *et al.* [FPG03]. Using AASE on top of such a layout, mapped to metrics like *number of bug reports* or *number of recent changes* offers a walkthrough in our software visualization were we simply hear about our critical hot spots. Thanks to ambient audio wound up a set of entities with a particular dependency, we get attentive as well as cases where small individual entities, because of their relation, represent a critical situation to a project component.

4.4.5 Case Study

To demonstrate our AASE concepts, we use a simple user study. The used ambient sound is similar to a bubble sound, everyone is familiar with from their daily life. We alter the volume and frequency based on the mapped software entities metrics. The bubble sound shows the different acoustic stages from still to boiling water. The higher the volume and frequency is, the more the perceived feedback resembles the one of boiling water.

For the case study, we use different versions of the Azureus 2 project[2]. The used evolutionary data set consists of 3 major releases from v3.0.5 to v3.1.1. The metrics were calculated per release. In the following, we demonstrate with a simple task how ambient audio exploration can help guiding the user to the relevant entities.

Figure 4.6 shows a Hotspot-View with all the packages of Azureus version 3.0.5 as explained in [BG07b]. In our case study, we simply look for packages including classes that were recently changed. Solving the task in a visual-only approach, would require to change the color mapping to show where changes were made. Ambient audio allows one to simply leaving the entities in the current color mapping and just move around the exploration marker, while listening to the audio feedback. If we move the exploration marker towards (a) in Figure 4.6 we hear an ambient sound similar to a soft sea, approaching (b) we perceive a more stormy ambient sound, and close to (c) the ambient sound resembles the one of boiling water. We can therefore argue that in (a) there where only little changes since the last release, some were made in (b), and quite a few changes were made to the classes in package (c).

---

[2]azureus.sourceforge.net last checked 14.1.2012

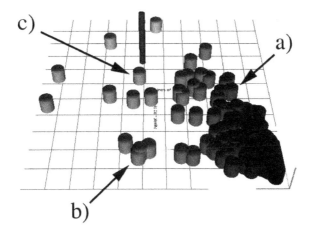

Figure 4.6: Hotspot view of the packages present in Azureus v3.0.5 with ambient audio exploration marker

4.5 Résumé

In this chapter, we presented two main approaches to support software visualization with an aural feedback. We validate these approaches in Part III.

With Entity Audio we intended to use an aural feedback to represent the characteristics of one particular software entity. It supports a visualization whenever an observer faces several entities and needs further information about them to complete his task. The aural feedback gets triggered by clicking on one particular entity or hovering over them with the mouse. When an audio notification gets triggered an algorithm calculates the feedback based on its metrics, the configured thresholds or value changes compared to previous releases.

Our ambient audio software exploration (AASE) approach guides an observer towards one particular software entity, based on the aural feedback representing the entities characteristics. It is intended to support a visualization whenever an observer faces several entities and needs combined information over several entities to complete his task. The aural feedback gets triggered in moving a virtual position marker around the visualization and listening to the aural feedback at this position. AASE particularly assists software visualizations investigation and perception of situations where individually irrelevant entities with dependencies become relevant.

5

Automating Tasks

In this chapter, we discuss how we can adequately integrate software visualizations in a general software engineering workflow. With an automated configuration approach, we intended to lower the threshold of using software visualization within software development and comprehension. The main idea is to simplify the use of software visualization for common situations in software comprehension. An important question among researchers therefore is, what common situations software engineers encounter during their general workflow. With our approach we present how to lower the steps a developer needs to take to adequately configure a software visualization for his common needs.

This chapter is structured as follows: In Section 5.1 we address the applicability of our automated tasks approach. Section 5.2 introduces various categories of common software comprehension tasks. Section 5.3 shows how we intend to simplify the configuration processes for a software visualization in our implementation.

5.1 Basics

The comprehension task approach explained in this chapter is built as part of a configuration framework for COCOVIZ. However, the idea behind using comprehension task to simplify the creation of visualization is not dependent on the COCOVIZ approach and can be used in combination with other visualizations.

5.2 Discovering Common Tasks

Our focus is to simplify the workflow in software comprehension with a seamless integration of software exploration concepts. An important factor to achieve this is to understand what engineers are looking for during their program comprehension tasks.

Several answers for such important program comprehension tasks are described in the work of Silito *et al.*, Alwis and Ferret, and Erdos [SMV06, SMV07, AM08, ES98].

For the purpose of our project, we took all the answered questions from those publications and added additional ones based on our personal experience. We categorized the catalog in five categories. Subsequently, we inspected them from a software exploration point of view and figured out, which ones are solvable with an automated comprehension task. In the following paragraph we discuss shortly the essence of the five categories we assembled.

1. Functionality. In our understanding, questions about functionality and location are related to finding software entities, attributes or an initial point in the code. These questions are often considered in program comprehension when engineers know little about the code or whenever they explore a new part of the system. Examples for this category are: *Where is a particular subroutine or procedure invoked?* [ES98], *Is there any method involved in the implementation of this behavior?* [SMV06].

2. Relationships of Code Entities. The relationship category combines the questions concerned with finding related software components. These questions are often used on a set of entities, such as methods, when an engineer aims to learn more about the entity itself and how it is used in the system. Example questions for this category are: *Who calls this method?* [AM08], *Does this entity have any siblings in the type hierarchy?* [SMV06].

3. Features and their Implementation. The feature category deals with understanding of concepts in the code that involve multiple relationships. Examples are: *How is this feature or concern implemented?* [SMV06]', *How does control-flow reach a particular location?*

4. Architecture and Design. These questions distinguishes themselves from the feature questions in that they deal with multiple subparts, whereas the *feature* questions focus on one subgraph only. Examples are: *What classes implement an interface?* [AM08], *What will be (or has been) the direct impact of this change?* [SMV06]

5. Testing. In the testing category, questions concern about assuring the implementation according to the requirements. Whenever a release gets to its final stage, engineers ask for help in finding entities or program components that need to be tested. Examples for this category are: *Are entities covered by any test? Which parts need more test coverage after a change?*

On top of that, the five major categories can further be divided into subgroups for more specific classifications such as *Code Smell Detection* within *Architecture and Design*. With these sets, an engineer finds his specific task quite easily without loosing time.

5.3 Architecture

To automate the configuration processes for the common tasks we built a dedicated framework. In the following, we describe the architecture of our automated comprehension task workflow. We explain the control routines used to create a software visualization (Figure 5.1) and describe adjustments to the workflow during software exploration (Figure 5.3). The numbering convention used in the Figures 5.1 and 5.3 is arbitrary and is used only for reference purpose.

5.3.1 Comprehension tasks control flow

Whenever an engineer starts software analysis (Figure 5.1 - the step numbered 100) a collection of available comprehension tasks is presented (Figure 5.2 left). After selecting a desired comprehension task (Step 110), the implementation of a task is called to analyze the dataset, as well as available statistics and metrics to create task specific entity groups (Step 111). For instance, if we look for code smells in methods, the task will possibly create at least an entity group with all the method entities in the dataset, whereas *Finding siblings* will possibly create at least an entity group including all the class entities with siblings. Based on the specific groups created, an engineer is presented with a filtered dataset that contains suggested entities to focus on (Step 112).

The engineer can select one of the suggested entity groups or focus the task on particular entities of this group (Figure 5.2 right). With the selection of the base entities for a task (Step 120), the software audio-visualization is created. The task first uses the selected base entities to filter the dataset and get all the entities for the visualization algorithms (Step 121). For instance, finding a *God class* as specified in [LM06]. If we select to focus the task on the entities in a package, the task will filter all class entities within that package that satisfies the rules for a *God class* code smell.

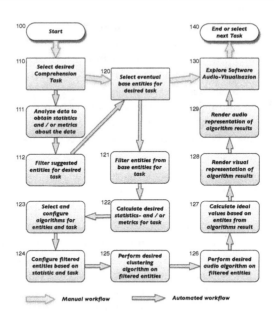

Figure 5.1: Comprehension Tasks Architecture

Based on the filtered entities the boundaries and special metrics are calculated eventually (Step 122). A task then specifies what algorithm applies for the creation of cognitive shapes. The algorithms for the shape colors, textures, and layouts are calculated. If present the calculation of an audio representation is performed. All the algorithms are then configured for the task (Step 123). For instance, in a task related to integration tests, a force-directed-algorithm is used to calculate the positions of the shapes. The algorithm is therefore configured to use the entity calls as edges, and to limit the number of iteration in the simulation. After all algorithms have been specified and configured, the entities get assigned a start position (Step 124). This is important for algorithms that require a specific or random distributed layout before performing the algorithm. For instance, the task on integration tests requires the entities to have a randomly assigned position before the algorithm is performed. In Step 125 all the configured algorithms are performed according to the comprehension task either sequentially, in a specific order or in parallel. If an audio algorithm is used it is performed in Step 126. Before rendering the results, the comprehension task calculates the optimal values for the result entities and eventually tags entities that will be suggested and specially presented to the engineer (Step 127).

In Steps 128 and 129 the final results are rendered to a visual and an aural representation. The boundaries for the used metrics are set based on the presented result entities. A software audio-visualization with interesting suggestions is shown to the engineer, ready to explore.

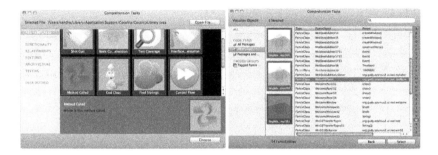

Figure 5.2: Automated workflow showing Step 110 (left) and Step 120 (right)

5.3.2 Comprehension tasks during software exploration

Whenever an engineer performs an interaction in the software exploration (Figure 5.3 - Step 210) the implementation of a current comprehension task recives a notification. The notification is evaluated and whenever an interaction requests a reconfiguration of a comprehension task or needs to recalculate the results of an algorithm, dedicated actions are taken. For example, an engineer changes the maximal value visible for a mapped metric *Number of Attributes* in the SV-Mixer [BG07b] (Step 240). The comprehension task is notified and recalculates the results of the algorithm, whenever the algorithm is affected by the changed metric (Step 241). In a case where only visual parameters are affected, no algorithms are re-executed, only the visual boundaries are updated (Step 127) and the representation is re-rendered. If the metric instead of its values is changed, for example from *Number of Attributes* to *Number of Accessor Methods* then the layout algorithm is affected by the change and needs to be updated. The layout algorithm configurations are updated and re-performed (Step 123).

Whenever an engineer changes the clustering (Step 250) or the audio algorithm (Step 260), then the complete algorithm needs to reexecute itself. The changed algorithms and filtered entities are reconfigured (Step 251 / 261) and the algorithm is reexecuted (Step 125 / 126).

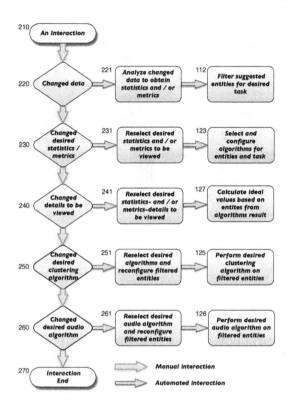

Figure 5.3: Changes during software exploration

If an engineer's interaction does not affect any relevant value for the comprehensions task, the control flow ends, and waits for the next interaction (Step 270).

5.4 Case Study

With the following case studies we demonstrate the applicability of automated comprehension tasks in software exploration. We select typical software comprehension use cases, and solve them with the help of automated tasks, then compare it to the effort needed to solve it with a non-automated approach.

In these examples we use a dataset consisting of 3 major releases (v3.0.5, v3.1.0 and v3.1.1) from the Azureus 2 project. The metrics were calculated for each release.

5.4.1 Functionality Comprehension Task

With our first software comprehension task, we address where the randomly selected method update in class DefaultSaveLocationmanager is invoked. For this purpose, we use the *Procedure Invocation* task found in the functionality task group (Figure 5.2 left). As we are looking for the update method, we select *All Methods* from the suggested entity group and type the method's name in the search field (similar Figure 5.2 right). The visualization is created and we get to see a cognitive comprehension visualization showing all the entities that invoke the update method. As familiar from a non-automated COCOVIZ approach, we explore the entities, their metrics and relations, select the most interesting ones and tag them for further tasks.

In a non-automated approach, we would have needed to: (1) select the method from the suggested entities page; (2) query the data-set for methods that invoke the update method; (3) configure the shapes for the visualization; (4) apply a position algorithm; (5) calculate the ideal metrics for the cognitive representation; and (6) focus the visualizations boundaries to the values of the presented entities. With the automated tasks we are now able to reduce the number of steps an engineer needs to do for software exploration from 6 to 2 steps.

5.4.2 Relationship Comprehension Task

The class DefaultSaveLocationmanager from our previous task seems to represent a default implementation of an interface. To verify that, we use the *Find Siblings* task under the relationships task group. On the suggested entities page we choose *Show All Classes* and select the DefaultSaveLocationmanager class. From this selection a visualization is created, where we perceive that our class under inquiry has in fact siblings such as the SaveLocationmanager. We can now tag the interesting siblings and continue our work.

In a non-automated approach we would have needed to: (1) select the method from the suggested entities page; (2) and (3) perform two queries to the data-set for sibling classes of `DefaultSaveLocationmanager`; (4) configure the shapes for the visualization; (5) apply a position algorithm; (6) calculate the ideal metrics for the cognitive representation; and (7) focus the visualizations boundaries to the values of the presented entities. In using the *Find Siblings* task we therefore reduce the number of steps an engineer needs to do software exploration from 7 to 2 steps.

5.4.3 Feature Comprehension Task

The previously described tasks were rather trivial tasks. If an engineer's interest is more in the features rather than use the `update` method, he probably will select the *Control Flow* task from the feature task group. There are two big differences compared to *Procedure Invocation*. First, the *Control Flow* task does not only query for the methods that invoke the `update` method, but also queryies recursively for the methods invoking those methods. Second, the task configures and performs a force-directed algorithm to position all the queried methods based on their invocation relationship. The result is a visual representation where methods are positioned closer, the stronger their relations are, and therefore we perceive a nice visualization of the control-flow around the `update` method. Again, we explore the result entities, tag, or examine them in detail.

In a non-automated approach, beyond the 6 steps needed for the *Procedure Invocation*, we would have needed to: (1) perform recursive queries for methods invoking `update`; (2) configure the force-directed algorithm; and (3) set a random start position for all the queried methods prior to performing the force-directed algorithm. In using the *Control Flow* task we therefore reduce the number of steps an engineer needs to do software exploration from 9 to 2 steps.

5.4.4 Design Comprehension Task

Whenever an engineer wants to know whether some code smells apply to a software component, he finds the dedicated tasks under the *Architecture* task group. For instance, if we would like to know what classes are affected by the God Class code smell symptoms in the `org.gudy.azureus2.core3.util`, we select the *God Class detection* task and focus on the mentioned package in the entity selection. The results are presented in a hot-spot visualization, where, entities base their shape metaphors (*e. g.* House-Metaphors) on their complexity and size metrics. The entity positions are mapped to *Number of Methods* (x-axes) and *Number of Attributes* (y-axes). We can then explore the `util` package and discovers intuitively the potential God Classes according to their position and size. Figure 5.4 depicts such a visualization in Azureus where we see classes with potential god class code smell symptoms: a) `DisplayFormatters`, b) `ThreadPool` and c) `TorrentUtils`.

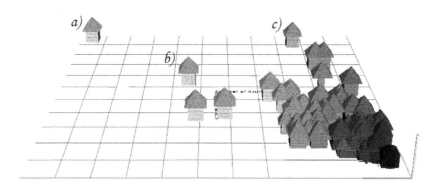

Figure 5.4: Hotspot view of the 'org.gudy.azureus2.core3.util' package in Azureus

In a non automated approach we would have needed to: (1) select the package from the suggested entities page; (2) perform a query for the classes within the package `org.gudy.azureus2.core3.util`; (3) configure the shapes for the visualization (4) apply a position algorithm; (5) calculate the ideal metrics for the cognitive representation; and (6) focus the visualizations boundaries to the values of the presented entities. In using the *God Class detection* task we therefore reduce the number of steps an engineer needs to do for software exploration from 6 to 2 steps.

5.4.5 Architecture Comprehension Task

If an engineer is further interested in where changes to the complexity of the system were made compared to the previous version, he selects the *Changed Complexity Audio* task. This task for the visual representation uses a hot-spot view and positions the entities with a force-directed algorithm according to their incoming call relation. Furthermore, an ambient audio algorithm is configured as explained before (Chapter 4), where volume and frequency are mapped to an entity's delta change in cyclomatic complexity compared to its previous version.

With this task we explore the software's visual and aural-representation in moving the audio-exploration marker around and listen to a surround sound composed of several bubble sounds getting louder and with a higher frequency the more changes happened to an entity. The perceived total sound however represents not only the aural-representation of one particular entity but the one of a set of strongly related entities. We therefore get notified which component of strongly related entities changed in complexity and can tag them according to our needs.

A non-automated approach besides the steps for 'Procedure Invocation' would further need: (1) configuring the position algorithm; (2) setting random start position for the entities, configuring; (3) and performing; (4) the audio algorithm. With the *Changed Complexity Audio* task we reduce the steps needed for software exploration from 10 to 2.

Tasks	# steps non automated	# steps automated
Procedure Invocation	6	2
Find Siblings	7	2
Control Flow	9	2
God Class	6	2
Changed Complexity	10	2

Table 5.1: Steps needed to do software exploration on common comprehension tasks

5.5 Résumé

Automated comprehension tasks are intended to simplify the creation of software visualizations for most common software comprehension tasks. The idea is that an engineer only needs to select the task he needs and a set of entities he wants to focus on to get a first visualization. These simplifications combined with a seemless integration of exploration concepts allows one to lower the threshold of using software visualization in the first place (Table 5.1) and offers a simple way to combine one task after the other, when dealing with complex workflows.

6
Tactile Approach

Tablets and multitouch interaction devices have found their way into industry and the consumer market during the last years. These tactile devices support a more natural interaction compared to the traditional mouse and keyboard input devices. In this chapter, we verify the usability of multitouch devices for software exploration. This tactile approach therefore is intended to push the audio-visual approach further towards a natural perception of virtual data. The main idea is to use tactile devices for a better interaction and navigation within a software visualization and improve communication in situations such as a code reviews where multiple observers work together.

We implemented the support for tactile devices, independent from our other approaches, with an extensible gesture framework.

The remainder of this chapter is structured as follows: In Section 6.1 we explain the basics of our tactile approach. Section 6.2 shows how we interconnected the tactile approach with the others in COCOVIZ. In Section 6.3 we explain useful gestures in a software visualization context.

6.1 Basics

The tactile approach explained in this chapter is built on the open standards TUIO[1]. This allows one to support several tactile devices and preserve independence from one particular device.

During our work we experimented with several devices from smaller monitors up to larger table tops. Therefore, we address the use of touch tables and gestures in software engineering in general, and discuss the benefits such devices can bring to a software project.

---

[1] www.tuio.org last checked 14.1.2012

6.2 Architecture

In COCOVIZ, we implemented the tactile functionality as additional dedicated controllers that interact with the main controllers of our Model-View-Controller-Architect [Ree79]. Whenever a user touches the multitouch-screen, a touch-event is generated and sent to the applications event-handler chain (Figure 6.1). The touch-event contains the coordinates where the touch happened on the screen, a unique id is used to distinguish multiple touches and the status of the touch. A touch-event has one of five possible states: touch-create, touch-down, touch-move, touch-up, touch-delete.

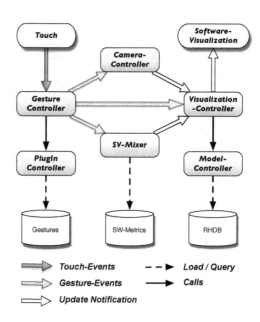

Figure 6.1: CocoViz: Multi-touch Architecture

A dedicated Gesture-Controller handles these touch-events. The Gesture-Controller has a set of registered gestures that are loaded at runtime and enabled or disabled according to the use case. Whenever a touch event occurs the gesture controller evaluates how many touches are active and passes the last touch event together with the older still active ones to the enabled and applicable gesture methods. A gesture event notification, containing all the relevant gesture information, is passed on to the application event handler. The gesture method checks if the active touches represent a gesture. If a gesture is detected a gesture method creates a gesture event. Classes within COCOVIZ can register for such specific gesture events and get notified whenever such an event occurs. There are three main-controllers that register for gesture-notification within the gesture-controller.

The Camera-Controller of the active software visualization registers for zoom gesture events. Whenever a zoom gesture occurs, the Camera-Controller gets notified and calculates the new zoom-factor with information from the gesture event before notifying the visualization controller to update the view.

The Metric Configurator registers for a swipe gesture (Figure 6.2 b) and notifies the entities when metric-filters are altered.

However, Visualization-Controllers can also register for gestures events themselves when gestures trigger visualization services. For instance, a four touch gesture in COCOVIZ is used to trigger an audio notification. The gestures for audio notifications are handled in the main Visualization-Controller. They call the model-controller to update changes in the dataset and redrawing the visualization.

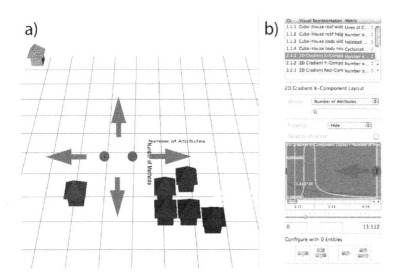

Figure 6.2: COCOVIZ with multi-touch support

6.3 Gestures

The capability of touching a multitouch-screen and notify the application components accordingly is one aspect. The more important aspect is to combine the right reaction to an observer's action. In the following, we discuss different gesture types and the mappings we found intuitive and useful in the context of software exploration and comprehension. The gestures are divided into three categories based on the fingers needed to trigger the gesture.

6.3.1 Gesture Mappings

When implementing a gesture, we have to ask ourself what action shall happen as a result to that gesture. How do we map the gestures to adequate actions. There are different approaches to discover gesture mappings. When looking at other multitouch implementations, we typically find common gestures used in almost every implementation such as a pinch or rotate. With a pinch-gesture an observer in a graphical context expects a zoom-in or zoom-out. It would not make sense to map those common gestures to completely different actions. An action to a gesture therefore needs to relate to the intuitive natural expectations of the user. To find possible intuitive mappings for a specific gestures where adequate mappings are not obvious in a special context, we conducted a user study. In the survey users associate a list of actions with a particular gesture. We addressed potential mappings for the gestures and evaluated what actions are considered more important and intuitive than others. An overview of the gestures used in our approach is found in Table 6.1.

6.3.2 Single-Touch Gestures

Single touch gestures are commonly used for pointing and navigating purposes. Their use is often much like that of a mouse. Nevertheless, there is a big difference when comparing a single touch on a touchscreen to a mouse move. With a mouse move can arrive simultaneously with a mouse button pressed. Therefore moving a mouse can trigger two different events. On a touchscreen, a move is only triggered if the screen is touched, there are no option keys altering the event. A multitouch input device therefore has only three trivial single-touch gestures: single-touch-down, single-touch-move, and single-touch-up. However, more sophisticated gestures are possible with a single touch. Most of these gestures use a bezier path pattern. Similar to writing letters, these gestures are triggered when a touch-move path resembles the predefined path.

In COCOVIZ we use the single-touch gesture for two purposes. When pointing at a software entity, the entity is selected and detailed information is presented in the inspector view (Figure 6.2 b). The input data is analyzed and inspected with further single-touches. The second purpose is to alter the version to visualize, apply and customize filters with the parameter sliders.

As a proof of concept we implemented more sophistic gestures. In our software exploration context, we considered **Single circle** and **Single wave** useful.

Single circle gesture is used to ask for details about a selected entity group and is triggered when touch-moving around the entities in a circle like path.

The **Single wave** gesture is intuitive to present a historical view on the selected entity. To trigger a historical view an observer would touch the entity followed by a sinus-wave like touch-move path.

6.3.3 Dual-Touch Gestures

With the emerging industrial multitouch devices, dual-touch gestures have been the most commonly used gestures. We find such devices in a movie with a futuristic plot or in broadcast television productions, during president dial elections for statistic analysis or simply to navigate on a virtual globe on a multitouch device. Dual-touch gestures are found particularly useful for graphical navigation. The zoom, rotate and swipe gestures represent an already familiar paradigm for most explorers. An explorer even expects a specific action. Therefore, we keep such familiar behavior in an adaption for software exploration.

Moving with two touches on the screen closer to each other therefore results in zooming closer to a certain software entity, meanwhile moving the touches farther away from each other ends up in zooming out and further away from a certain entity. When rotating two touches around a common center an observer expects to rotate the current visualization. Depending on the situation in a three dimensional context, the gesture triggers a rotation of the camera either around its own axis or around a central point of interest. In our context, we calculate the delta change of the rotation in a radial format and rotate the camera around the selected software entity. When no entity is selected, the center of the visualization is taken as the rotation origin.

Whenever an observer uses two touches to slide them to the same direction, he usually expects a page up/down notification. In the software exploration context, we do not have pages. We therefore use the delta change in distance of such a swipe gesture to adjust the camera horizontal position (Figure 6.2a). With this mapping, we can zoom, rotate and move the camera along a visualization with two fingers. We further use more sophisticated dual touch gestures. The control touch gesture is intended to simulate a right mouse button to trigger a context menu for compatibility reasons. The control touch gesture is triggered with one finger touching the screen and not being moved and a second touching the screen to the right. The second touch then resembles a virtual click on a right mouse button (Figure 6.3).

A wave gesture with two touches, would make sense to trigger an analyzes with regard to historical changes. We found a comparison of two or more selected entities with regard to their history an adequate mapping. The gesture path itself resembles one of two parallel sinus-waves.

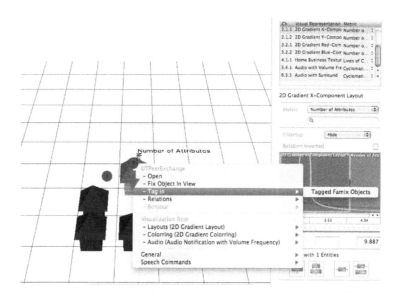

Figure 6.3: A control drag gesture in CocoViz

6.3.4 Multitouch Gestures

We refer to multitouch gestures when more than two fingers at the same time are used to touch a multitouch sensitive surface. Multiple gesture combinations are possible. To investigate its practicality in software exploration, we implemented simple three-touch- and four-touch gestures that suit our purpose.

In our context we use three touches to move a software entity independently to its layout and to preserve it, even when a visualization changes its filters or visible entity. One might think of a bookmark like functionality. It resembles the act of taking a chess figure from the chessboard, but preserving it next to the board for later comparison. We triggered this behavior in touching the entity of interest with one touch to select it, followed by two more fingers touching the screen. The interaction resembles the normal behavior of pointing at the top of a chess figure and garbing it with two more fingers to move it around. The entity is than moved to the new location in the view without changing the other entities (Figure 6.4).

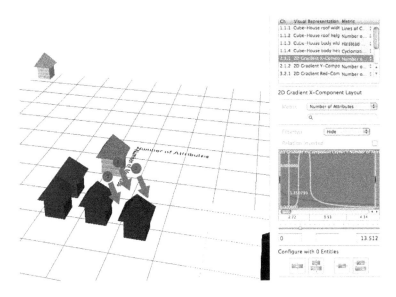

Figure 6.4: Moving an entity like a chess figure with three fingers

To directly access an ambient audio source [BG08], we use four fingers touching he surface at the same time. Touching the screen with four fingers brings up an exploration marker. The exploration marker represents an observer's position in the visualization space. It visualizes the position from where the observer listens to the audio notification. Moving with four fingers around the touch surface is like the natural behavior of grabbing the exploration marker with four fingers and moving it to a new position. While the marker is moved around in the visualization, the audio controller gets notified of the new position and changes the played audio representation accordingly. The observer perceives the audio notification corresponding to the new position and can adequately adjust his navigation in the visualization. (Figure 6.5).

Touches	Gestures	Actions
Single-Touch		
↕↔	Click	Select Entity
↻	Circle	Entity Details
∿→	Wave	Evolutionary View
Dual-Touch		
↺	Rotate	Rotate View
↕↔	Swipe	Rotate View Camera
↗↙	Pinch	Zoom-In / Out
• ↕	Control-Drag	Context-Menu
Multi-Touch		
↓↓↗	Three-touch	Move an Entity
↕↔	Four-touch	Ambient Audio

Table 6.1: Overview of the multi-touch gestures

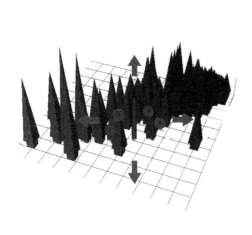

Figure 6.5: Moving an audio exploration marker like a chess figure with four fingers

6.4 Case Study

In the following, we show the applicability of touch screen technologies combined with 3D software visualization during a software review. We show how collaboration benefits from multitouch techniques during common software comprehension tasks and how to discuss solutions while exploring a software visualization. To demonstrate the applicability of our idea, we use COCOVIZ in a version suitable for multitouch tables.

6.4.1 Setup of Experiment

Our COCOVIZ version suitable for multitouch tables offers support for different multitouch devices. We support TUIO [KBBC05] compatible multitouch screens based on FTIR [Han05] such as our self-made multitouch table[2] through the opentouch[3], an open source framework for multimodal input devices. Furthermore, we

---

[2]http://www.sdfb.ch/de/projekte/edit last checked 14.1.2012
[3]http://code.google.com/p/opentouch last checked 14.1.2012

support stantum multitouch devices with an implementation of the Stantum's SDK[4]. These frameworks generate touch events containing the coordinates where the finger touched the screen, along with a unique id to distinguish multiple touches and the status type of the touch (touch-down, touch-move, touch-up) are handled by COCOVIZ's Gesture-Controller.

6.4.2   A Collaboration Scenario

To demonstrate the implications of touch screen technology on software visualization, the following section transcribes a typical software review involving two software engineers (Alex and Laura) discussing issues with the current generation of their software system.

Context: Assume Alex and Laura are engineers of a commercial web framework. We find them during a software review, discussing about problematic parts of the design and the impact planned changes may have on the stability of their next software release.

Alex and Laura are both familiar with the software architecture and use COCOVIZ as a discussion platform. They start their review by looking at a general overview of the system components. They use the Hotspot-View representing the entities based on their complexity and size metrics. To focus on interesting entities they adjust the sliders in the SV-Mixer view with their finger and filter currently unused entities out (Figure 6.2b).

3D exploration: By touching with their fingers on the screen, they move the camera of the 3D software visualization around and explore the software project. For this purpose, they can use most gestures that they are already familiar from multitouch-capable mobile phones and trackpads, such as point, swipe, pinch, and zoom.

Audio exploration: Laura is asking Alex whether an error-prone class she uses in her code was changed since the last review. To explore that class, she tips on the glyph representing the class and can show Alex the detailed information in the inspector view. Furthermore, they can use an entity audio notification to get aural feedback on the changes that class had over the last revisions.

Touch screen manipulation: Alex is not sure whether the fixes made to the class would solve Laura's problem but suggests to have a detailed look at the code later on. To keep track of the class he tags the class with a *two touch-drag* gesture.

Alex points at a complex, large class represented as a big house, and decides to keep this potential god class in mind for a discussion on stability of the next release. He touches the class with one finger and then uses two more fingers to move the entity to a fixed position aside all the other entities (*three touch-drag* gesture).

---

[4]http://www.stantum.com last checked 14.1.2012

Identify high Impact changes: Laura suggest to check stability on other similar classes by checking large classes (larger than 200 lines of code) with high complexity (*e. g.* cyclomatic complexity [McC76]). Such classes often incorporate a remarkable amount of system functionality. She argues, that if such a class was changed since the last release, there is potential for a high impact on the overall system.

She configures the view to show only large classes with more than 200 lines of code, filters out classes with lower complexity, and configures the ambient audio notification with an algorithm from the audio menu (*e. g. historical audio*). Now that ambient audio notification is configured, she can touch the screen with four fingers and bring up the ambient audio exploration marker (Figrue 6.5). In moving the four fingers on the touchscreen, she moves the exploration marker around and listens to the audio feedback. Moving towards the different entities, they hear a sound similar to a calm sea for few changes, more stormy sound for light changes and a sound that resembles the one of boiling water for a lot of changes.

Based on these findings they can tag the entities with a lot of changes for further investigation with a *two touch-drag* gesture or move them to a fixed position aside the others as explained before (*tree touch-drag*) and continue with their review.

6.5 Résumé

The use of tactile devices represents a basic component for an intuitive and natural perception of software. The idea is to combine a cognitive comprehensible visualization together with a intuitive tactile navigation and on top of that supporting the visual impression with an aural perception. This allows us to experience software closer to our natural way of exploring things. Just as a child learns about an environment by listening, looking, and touching the objects surrounding it. We present the validation in Part III.

7

Speech Approach

The speech approach in COCOVIZ is intended to support tactile interaction when exploring a software system and give spoken feedback when otherwise appropriate. While exploring a software system we find ourselves often in situations where we look for particular objects, such as a starting point or we have to combine particular tasks together. This may require typing on the keyboard. In a tactile situation that means using a rather uncomfortable virtual keyboard on the touch table. With the use of spoken commands we show how to reduce the accesses to a virtual keyboard. This chapter is structured as follows: We start explaining the basics of our speech approach in Section 7.1. We present the architecture for speakable commands and how we leveraged the benefits of our automated comprehension tasks with these speakable commands in Section 7.2.

7.1 Basics

Over the years, speech recognition was strongly improved and found its way into commercial products. Its accuracy still has limitations when it comes to recognize full sentences. Often, intensive voice training is needed to improve the voice recognition. If the commands to recognize are specified, however the accuracy is enough to use in common situations. An example for the use of speech recognition in common situations can be found in technologies such as Siri used in mobile devices[1]. We investigated its use in combination with our tactile approach. The command oriented speech recognition used in this chapter is build on top of the *NSSpeechRecognizer* APIs, a part of the standard Mac OS X 10.3 and later[2]. The speakable commands are defined as part of COCOVIZ's general interaction. Some dedicated

---

[1]http://www.apple.com/iphone/features/siri.html last checked 14.1.2012
[2]http://developer.apple.com/mac/library/navigation/index.html last checked 14.1.2012

methods in our frameworks provide further extension points. For instance, we access the automated comprehension tasks in simply speaking the tasks name.

7.2 Architecture

The speech support in COCOVIZ is accessed with a dedicated Speech-Controller. The controller handles both speakable command recognition and the synthesis of spoken text output.

The main methods of the speech-controller are *setSpeechControls:* and *addSpeech-Controls:*. Both take a list of speakable command strings as input parameters. The first method overwrites the available commands with the new ones, whereas the second method adds the new commands to the already active ones. In COCOVIZ the OpenChooser uses the speech-controller quite intensively. The OpenChooser is the frontend of our automated task approach. When creating a software visualization, it queries the plugin-controller for the available comprehension tasks and loads the speakable commands of every task into the speech-controller. Combined with some basic entity selection and filter commands they are added and removed to the speech-controller dynamically based on the usability during the current step.

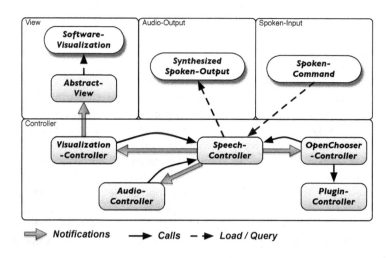

Figure 7.1: Speech architecture in COCOVIZ

Whenever an observer uses a speakable command the speech-controller notifies the addressed controller. The OpenChooser-controller or the visualization-controller can than address the needed actions for this particular command.

The speech controller class defines as well a singleton instance called defaultSpeech-Controller. This allows to access the speak-synthesizer from every extension that needs spoken text output. For instance, in an entity audio algorithm analyzing potential code smell patterns, we use this feature to give an oral feedback to an observer on whether the entity under discussion is a potential god class or not. The audio algorithm simply analyzes an entity and sends a composed string of its result to the defaultSpeechController's *taskSpeechCommand:* method. The method takes a string as parameter and synthesizes a spoken output.

7.3 Case Study

With the following case studies, we present a common software exploration situation where our speech approach is applicable in combination with tactile interfaces. We show how the use of spoken commands allows us to eliminate the need to access a keyboard to solve a software exploration task on a multitouch table and confirm the Hypotheses 4a discussed in Section 1.3. To demonstrate the applicability, we use COCOVIZ on a multitouch table.

Context: The context is the same used in the case study on tactile devices (Section 6.4). We assume again that Alex and Laura are engineers during a software review discussing problematic parts of their next software release.

Alex and Laura are both familiar with the software architecture and use COCOVIZ as a discussion platform. They start their review by looking at a general overview of the system components. An Hotspot-View shows them the software entities based on their complexity and size metrics.

Software exploration: By touching with their fingers on the screen, they move the camera of the 3D software visualization around and explore the software project. For this purpose, they can use most gestures that they are already familiar from multitouch-capable mobile phones and trackpads, such as point, swipe, pinch, and zoom.

Laura is asking Alex about updates on an error-prone class in their network framework, that she uses in her code. To explore that class, she needs to find the class in the visualization. Without speech commands this involves either a filtering of classes (*e.g.* show only large classes with more than 200 lines of code) or search for the class name or another characteristic of the class. To filter classes with more than 200 lines of code on a multitouch table, they need to show the filter view and move the minimum slider for lines of codes to 200. To search for the class name on a multitouch table, they need to write the name in the search field. This involves the use of a keyboard. On multitouch devices the use of a fiscal or virtual keyboard is inconvenient and time-consuming.

Speech commands: With our speech approach however, an observer in such a situation gets a simpler and faster solution. To find the error-prone class in our scenario Laura can say *Select class named networkcontroller* or *Select classes with metric lines of code greater 200*. In this scenario the use of our speech approach completely eliminates the need to access a multi-touch keyboard and enables a smoother workflow on a multi-touch device. If Laura does not remember the class name, she can use an automated comprehension task and say *Select class implementing framework network*, or *Select god classes*.

Thanks to the speech command the class gets selected in the code and no keyboard needs to be used. Laura can explore the entities for further investigation or move them to a fixed position beside the others as explained before (*tree touch-drag*) and continue with their review.

With this use case, we were able to use spoken commands in software exploration on a multitouch table to eliminate the need to access a keyboard to solve the task.

With regard to our Hypothesis 4a, we can conclude that spoken commands can be used to lower the need to access a keyboard during software exploration on a multitouch table.

7.4 Résumé

In this chapter, we extended COCOVIZ to use basic speech recognition and speech synthesis where appropriate. In fact we only considered the opportunities that arise in our interactive context when extending the approach with a list of speakable commands. Nevertheless, we were able to use these speakable commands as one solution to lower the need of accessing a virtual keyboard on a tactile device during a software comprehension task.

8

Collaborative Exploration

Most software visualization solutions focus on improving the perception of a software system or on helping to solve a particular task. This is useful, whenever an engineer is not familiar with the software and learns about important system components. During maintenance however, an engineer is worried more about the changes made to a component over time, and the impact a certain change will have to the system. For that he will tag an interesting entity found in the visualization and ask the engineer owning the code for further details. The engineer involved with that particular code fragment can explain the details about earlier design decisions, current bugs, or planned changes to that part of the code. Software analysis can help in several situations, still the engineers knowledge remains hard to capture. When we consider maintenance in medium to large software projects, we therefore have to adequately involve the whole project team.

Software visualization in general helps understanding present situations and offers a communication base among people from different domains. Our goal is to provide an adequate visualization to improve the collaboration among project teams.

We present two main situations, where software visualization can support collaboration. In the first use case, engineers and managers from different fields meet for a code review, a project meeting or even an audit. In the second use case, we address how to inform semantically related team members as early as possible about changes. They need to informed about component changes relevant to them.

The remainder of this chapter is structured as follows: In Section 8.1 we explain basic concepts were collaborative work can benefit from software visualization. Section 8.2 discusses use cases where engineers sit together and decide about future actions. Meanwhile Section 8.3 presents our solutions to improve informing related team members about changes.

8.1 Basics

Our goal is to support the collaboration between engineers involved in a development or maintenance project. To improve this collaboration, we have to think about the gaps in existing collaboration efforts. It is further important to understanding the relationship of the code you own yourself and actions within the software project. Whitehead [Whi07] in his work on collaboration in software engineering identified deficiencies in collaboration support. He sees important directions to improve software engineering's collaboration in better integrating the desktop-based IDE into the world wide web. According to Whitehead further enhancement to project collaboration are possible towards multi-project and multi-organization collaboration and in tools for capturing project-specific design trade-offs.

COCOVIZ is not a web-based IDE. Still, with the automated comprehension tasks, we worked on a closer integration of software visualization to the IDEs. And even with regard to multi-project and multi-organizational collaboration, our cognitive software visualization, with its graphical source code representation offers code independent discussion and comparison opportunities.

8.2 Collaboration on a touchtable

Collaboration is about people working together on a subject and share information. How this is adequately achieved is still subject of intensive studying. In the software exploration context, our COCOVIZ users see promising benefits when using multi-touch in a software review scenario. On a touch table participating stakeholders can commonly explore the system. In particular, the advantage of all sitting around the multi-touch table and having eye contact during the discussion as well as all having equality access to the controls are beneficial for collaboration.

To understand why a multitouch table offers advantage when collaboration involves people from different working areas, we observed users not always familiar with computers at an exhibition of our multi-touch project. Those users seemed to encounter few challenges and interacted with an unfamiliar application right away. In comparison, similar users in front of a monitor using a mouse to select objects often encounter more challenges.

To sustain these statements, we searched for literature addressing such a collaborative context.

Hilliges *et al.* describe a paradigm shift from human-computer interaction to computer-mediated human-to-human interaction [HTB+07]. They state that using a classical single-user systems in a collaborative setting, leads in most cases to a communication breakdown. The reasons for this is that the user's concentration shifts away from the group and towards the computer in order to use it.

Rodden *et al.* discovered that in existing computer support, the physical layout of technology can inhibit the interactions between the parties involved [RRHT03].

Stewart *et al.* performed a study on supporting social aspects in an environment with collaborators sharing the same part of the workspace. They pointed out how projects often benefit from group activity and input on a shared workspace, but also stated that the restrictive nature of current traditional systems can limit expression [SBD99].

Resnick *et al.* addressed the creativity support on multi-touch user-interfaces. They stated that the intuitive usage of a touch, lowers the threshold to get started with an application [RMK⁺05]. Shen describes how a user meeting around a touch table encourages collaboration, coordination, serendipity, as well as simultaneous and parallel interaction among multiple people [She07].

CoCoViz on a multitouch tables takes advantage of graphical metaphors and the benefit of an intuitive interaction. Together with a communication platform this allows participants an equally distributed interaction. Based on our observations and literature survey, we conclude that using a multi-touch table combined with software visualization offers high potentials in a collaborative environment such as a software review [BG10].

8.3 Mobile collaboration

Sharing relevant information in a software context, means get informed about important changes involving the own codebase and inform others about their emerging risks.

Within a project group, sharing of relevant information usually is done during meetings, along the working day, at lunch, in the cafeteria, or with emails. Depending on the importance of the situation, informing somebody with an email might not be enough. In critical situations, we have to make sure the involved engineer are noticed as soon as possible. Think of common situations where we forget to inform the other engineers about changes affecting them or we just do not know the involved engineers at all.

We need to find solutions that prevent forgetting to inform involved engineers. In CoCoViz we found a visual oriented solution to this issue. The ability to tag objects combined with push notification services allows a semi-automated notification service with independent preferences. If we further use mobile devices, we can push notification and inform involved people even faster when relevant changes arrive.

Imagine a situation where you have to change a software component, but you do not understand the impact this change will make on dependent components you have no influence on. You have to inform the involved parties about their emerging risk. In COCOVIZ, you can tag the components you are changing. We than apply software analysis on the tagged software entities and adequately notify the involved parties when relevant results are found.

8.3.1   Architecture

Our notification approach is based on a client-server approach (Figure 8.1). On every commit to a project repository, we analyze the changes and calculate the metrics used for software exploration. For this part, we rely on the evolizer project [GFP09] that stores the data to a release history database [FPG03]. After the new analysis is completed the notification controller is informed. The notification controller checks the entities that have been tagged for notification during software exploration. For the tagged entities that were changed our notification system than pushes adequate change notifications.

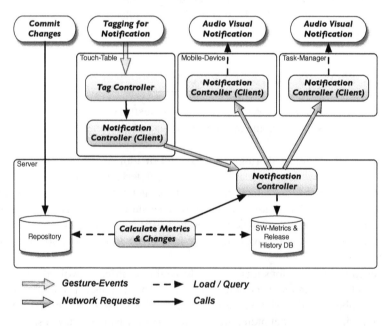

Figure 8.1: Model of our mobile collaboration implementation

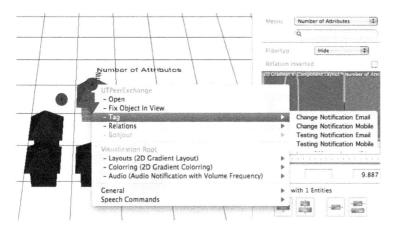

Figure 8.2: Tagging any software entity helps to remember or to inform a project member.

8.4 Case Study

With the following case studies, we present common situations where our mobile collaboration approach is applicable. We show how collaboration during these software maintenance tasks benefits when using software exploration in combination with mobile notification. To demonstrate the applicability, we use COCOVIZ on a multitouch table and a prototype of a mobile version.

Context: Assume Alex and Laura are engineers during a software review discussing problematic parts and the impact some planned changes will have on the stability of their next software release.

Since the last meeting, Alex encountered a bug in a framework he depends on but has no influence on. Together they explore the situation on the multitouch-table. As they have no direct way to contact the framework owner, they decide to file a bug report for that project and that in the meantime, Alex solves the bug with a workaround. By the time the bug in the framework gets fixed, he probably will have forgotten about the workaround and its potential risk. In our mobile collaboration environment, he can request an asynchron notification that will remember him about this situation when the event arrives. To schedule such a notification he just needs to tag the framework entity for with a change notification and decide whether he likes to be notified with an email or on his mobile device. The change notification for that particular framework is than added to his personal code watch list. By the time that

Figure 8.3: Example of a notification informing a project member

particular framework gets updated, he will be reminded with an email that he has to check this particular component again.

Laura on the other side is working on another class. She shows Alex on the multitouch-table that several parties from other groups are using the particular class. Because of the crucial situation, they decide that involved parties have to be informed about this change. Unfortunately, they do not know all the involved engineers. However, with our mobile notification approach they do not need to address involved engineers directly. It is enough to tag the class for a required testing notification. The notification requests are than added to the dependent parties watch lists and the system will asynchronly notify the involved engineers using the class Laura has changed (Figure 8.3).

During the review, they decide that Laura should wait with the change on the crucial class until Alex has fixed the framework bug. Because it is an important task, Laura wants to make sure she gets informed. To make sure she gets informed even if Alex forgets about her, she adds the component Alex will work on to her mobile watch list. By the time Alex commits his changes, she will get automatically notified on here mobile phone.

8.5 Résumé

In this chapter, we investigated how software visualization can improve collaboration within a project. In the first use case, we discussed benefits the use of COCOVIZ on a multitouch table towards collaboration in the context of a software review. In the second part, we presented the basic implementation of a visual oriented notification service, capable to inform involved parties on relevant changes on their preferred device such as a mobile device.

With these two basic approaches, we showed how software visualization can support a software project workflow.

Part III

Evaluation

In this part we focus on the validations of our approaches. For that we aim at testing the hypotheses of this thesis presented in Section 1.3.

The goal is to assess the various areas of our thesis as independent as possible and combine the results to address the applicability of the overall approach for an efficient software visualization. We do that with case studies and with a survey that we designed and conducted to cover also the psychological relevant areas. Where applicable we further support the hypothesis with case studies and take other research studies into consideration.

In Chapter 9 we address the design of our survey to cover the various hypothesis.

In Chapter 10 we deal with the results we found after running our survey.

9

Experimental Design

An experiment is supposed to evaluate an approach towards its applicability, usability, effectiveness and efficiency to a specific scenario. There are various ways to achieve such a goal. A good introduction to the various methods can be found in Robert K. Yin's Book on Case Study Research [Yin94]. In this thesis we evaluate the components of our approach with a survey addressing the different aspects independently.

9.1 Controlled Variables

Most of our approaches are not only linked to software and can be considered applicable to other domains as well. Therefore, the evaluation of our approaches is seen independently from software engineering wherever possible. Another argument is that in several situations, software projects involve individuals not familiar with programming at all (*e. g.* member of the contracting entity).

Considering these aspects, we focused on the background of our participants and their level of expertise towards software engineering and programming. The survey investigated information regarding years of experience in object-oriented programming, Java, and programming in general.

9.2 The survey

Because of the psychological background we rely on with each component of our approach, we decided to base the evaluation on a survey addressing the different aspects independently. Primarily the survey focuses on the visual approach, the aural approach, and the tactile approach.

For the visual approach, our goal was to understand what kind of self interpretation a user has when observing cognitive glyphs. In particular, we looked at whether an observer of a cognitive software visualization would understand the metaphors of a well-shaped house compared to a miss-shaped house. However, we did not only want to see, whether they understood such a metaphor as intended. We were also interested in how they interpreted other aspects along with it. In particular, we thought about situations, in which an observer miss-interprets a cognitive glyph, because he sees a beautiful artwork instead of a miss-shaped house. We addressed this in asking the participants of our survey to look at various glyphs without telling them anything with regard to the visualized data and let them tell us about their interpretations of the glyphs. The participants were able to choose from a set of adjectives and their opposites placed along a scale ranging from one to nine. They were intended to select one of these options, depending on whether they interpreted the presented glyph stronger adhering to the first adjective (one) or more related to its opposite adjective (nine). They where given a further option for the case they would not link any of the two adjectives to the glyphs.

For the aural approach, we divided the survey in three types of question groups. The first group similar to the visual part targeted the observers' interpretation. We did so in presenting different audio samples from our approach. In particular, we chose three samples from our audio metaphor: calm sea, light sparkling, and boiling water. Additionally, we took samples of other acoustic metaphors as a control group. The participants where asked to listen to the audio sample and then adhered their interpretation to a selected set of adjectives and their opposites.

In the second set of survey questions on audio, we focussed on the mapping of evolutionary data on aural feedback. We created four audio samples based on our entity audio approach. The samples were composed of 3 to 4 bass tunes each one representing a software entity and its evolutionary changes. The overall question was, whether an observer interpreted changes in the tones in line with the evolutionary changes of the data. The audio samples represented different software entities. One with constant increase, one with constant decrease, one with and increase and later decrease and one with a decrease and later increase back to the starting level.

The third set of survey questions related to audio, focused on our ambient audio approach. We looked at whether the participants understood audio as a guiding instrument towards entities of interest. In the online survey we do so in presenting them with a software visualization where we marked four places with a batch and a number from one to four. The participants were able to listen to four sound samples corresponding to the audio feedback an observer would hear at the marked places. We asked the participants towards which marked place they would lead the mouse if they were looking for a particular entity (*e. g.* an entity that had recent changes).

For our tactile approach, we aimed at understanding what action users would naturally expect as an result to a gesture on a multittouch table. The idea is to see whether a software visualization on a multitouch table can simplify the interaction with an intuitive user experience. In the survey we illustrated the participants software visualizations along with a multitouch gesture. We then asked our participants to attribute their expected actions to a multitouch gesture.

With the support of the survey, we were able to look for significant results within every single approach. Therefore, further research can build on top of every single approach independently.

9.3 Experiments

We ran the experiment over multiple phases, from mid 2010 to early 2011 (Table 9.3). Our first runs consisted of pilot sessions with computer science master students from our university. In these pilot sessions, the students all sat in the same class room. However they had to solve the surveys independently. Only marginal help was given, where problems resulted from the general understanding of a question. Out of these phases, we collected first results and used the valuable feedback for some changes to the survey with regard to an improved understandability.

Survey Type	Participants	Timeframe
Preliminary Survey	17 Participants	14.4.-28.5.2010
1st Public Survey	32 Participants	6.1.-18.1.2011
2nd Public Survey	37 Participants	19.1.-21.1.2011

Table 9.1: Participants overview of the conducted surveys

With the improved survey we addressed our public evaluation phase. The participants of our public evaluation had mostly an academic background but not necessarily all in software engineering. They were all unexperienced users with respect to our approaches. The demography showed a wide distribution across ages and fields of studies or occupations (Table 9.3). We opened this focus of our participants, because the essence of our study relies in a general psychological related perception and interaction of audio-visualization components. The results are not limited to a software development related area. Still, to collect a participants knowledge in software engineering, during the introduction of the survey we asked them about their profession and their experience with regard to object-oriented programing, java, the use of the Ecliple IDE and reverse engineering. Table 9.3 shows the demography of our survey participants with regards to their age and whether they have any knowledge in programming.

Survey Type	Age	Programming Knowledge
Preliminary Survey	23 Y - 32 Y	17 of 17 Participants
1. Public Survey	19 Y - 66 Y	9 of 32 Participants
2. Public Survey	17 Y - 56 Y	22 of 37 Participants

Table 9.2: Demography overview of the conducted surveys

In the first public survey the chronology of the survey was to first address the questions on the visual approach, second the aural approach and third the tactile approach. However during the first public survey, we realized that starting the survey with the visual approach would confuse several participants. Most of the confused participants reported that they felt like they would fall into cold water and would have been grateful for advice. We therefore changed the chronology of the survey to help the participants familiarize themselves with a software visualization of our tool. We did so in addressing the tactile questions first, as they showed several screen shots of software visualizations. In the second public survey the chronology of the survey therefore was to first address the questions on the tactile approach, second the aural approach and third the visual approach. The survey is included in Appendix A.

After an introduction the main survey started with six questions concerning our multitouch approach. Details and results are presented in Section 10.1. It moved on with eleven questions to our aural approach. The eleven questions were divided into four categories. The first category consisted of three questions to our entity audio approach (Section 10.2). The participants listened to a sound sample representing water in different phases. One sample with still water, one with blubbering water and one with boiling water. After every sample the participants were confronted with a set of adjectives with which they had to describe the sound samples. In the second category they were listening to two completely different sounds. One was an electric noise and one the start of a motor engine. These sounds were intended to be control questions with regard to the water samples. Again the participants had to describe the samples in their perception. In the third audio category we played four short melodies with a bass instrument. Each one consisted of four music notes. In one sample all the music notes increased, in one sample the notes decreased, in one sample the notes first increased and then decreased and in the last sample the notes decreased first and then increased. The participants were asked, what change over the last releases they would expect from an entity represented by such a sound sample. The fourth audio category had two questions on our ambient audio approach. We showed a software visualization with marked points. The participants had the opportunity to listen to sound samples that would be heard at the marked positions. We asked them to look for entities with a lot of changes in the past. Based on the sample they heard, they answered, towards which marked position they would go and expect entities with a lot of changes.

The visual approach was addressed after the audio approach. It consisted of four questions. The first three questions focused on the cognitive glyphs. In each question we showed a different house. The participants were confronted with a set of complementary adjectives, they had to describe the shaped house. In the fourth question, we compared the cognitive glyphs with other similar approaches. The participants were first presented software visualizations of the two approaches and then a shaped house along with a comparable visualization of the entity in the other approach. This time the participants had to select whether the shaped house or the comparable approach would better adhere to the set of adjectives.

The end of the survey consisted of a set of questions providing us with some feedback about the subject.

10

Results

In this chapter we present results of the survey we conducted to evaluate the components of our approach and confirm the hypotheses discussed in Section 1.3. The survey design and the performed experiments are presented in Chapter 9 and the survey is found in Appendix A.

10.1 Results for the Tactile Approach

With the result from our survey with regard to multitouch gestures, we concluded that tactile interfaces indeed can be used to support the interaction during software exploration. We address our Hypothesis 3b (Section 1.3), where we state that the use of multitouch permits an intuitive exploration in a three dimensional software visualization with minimal introduction overhead. In testing every gesture needed to do an adequate software exploration, we further verify our other Hypothesis 3a (Section 1.3), where we state that multitouch gestures mapped to navigation and interaction commands adequately enable software exploration. In the following we present the results from our multitouch related survey questions.

10.1.1 MQ1: Dual-touch move gesture

MQ1 showed a picture with a gesture, where two fingers would be placed together on the tactile surface and moved in parallel (Figure 10.1). In Section 6.3.3 we referred to it as a dual-touch move gesture. The participants were presented eight possible actions that could happen from the shown gesture (Table 10.1.1). Each action had nine possibilities to answer. If the participants were expecting an action to occur from this gesture, they would answer anything from the scale of one to four. If they were unsure the answer was five and if they would never expect this action from the gesture anything from six to nine. For the dual-touch gesture shown in MQ1 (Figure 10.1), we expected users would apply an action related to a change of camera or a change of position.

Zoom
Rotate
Context
Layout change
Change the position of the view camera
Show detail view
Show evolutionary view
Layout independent positioning of an Object

Table 10.1: Actions following a shown gesture

Calculation: We took the answers for each of our presented eight multi-touch actions seperately. We then categorized the answers for each action on a nominal scale. All answers from one to four build a first category and the answers from six to nine build a second category. To test the results for significant answers, we used chi-square tests.

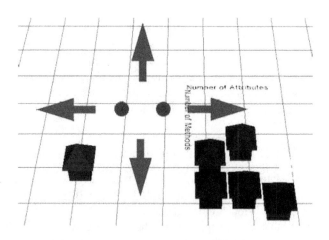

Figure 10.1: View presented in MQ1

> Change the position of the view camera
> $(\chi^2(1) = 14.000, p < .001)$.

Table 10.2: Significant actions expected for a dual-touch move gesture

Results: The results for MQ1 showed that significantly more participants answered that the action 'change the position of the view camera' was appropriate for the shown gesture (Table 10.2). The study showed as well that significantly more participants answered that the actions 'Rotate', 'Context', 'Show detail view' and 'Show evolutionary view' were not appropriate for the shown gesture (Table 10.3).

> Rotate
> $(\chi^2(1) = 10.286, p < .001)$.
> Context
> $(\chi^2(1) = 10.286, p < .001)$.
> Show detail view
> $(\chi^2(1) = 4.571, p < .05)$.
> Show evolutionary view
> $(\chi^2(1) = 4.571, p < .05)$.

Table 10.3: Significant not expected actions for a dual-touch move gesture

Conclusion: For MQ1 we can say that the participants' expectations of actions following from a given gesture were in line with our expectations and intuitively understood the shown dual-touch move gesture.

10.1.2 MQ2: Control drag gesture

MQ2 showed a gesture, where the first finger would be touched on a fixed position and the second one would than be moved to the right side (Figure 10.2). In Section 6.3.3 we referred to it as a control drag gesture. The intention of this gesture is to present a settings menu. However, the gesture is not a trivial gesture and we have as well not found any similar gestures in any other applications. We were not sure, about whether users would expect a menu as a result to such a gesture.

Calculation: The answers for each action were again categorized on a nominal scale. Two categories where built for each action, with one category including the answers from one to four and one category including the answers from six to nine. We then used chi-square tests to analyse the results for significant answers.

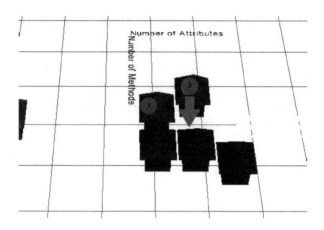

Figure 10.2: View presented in MQ2

For MQ2 the results indeed did not showed a clear significance in favor of one gesture. A reason might be that the gesture is not trivial to explain with a picture and therefore users did not understood how to use the gesture at all.

Layout change
$(\chi^2(1) = 3.267, p = .071)$.
Layout independent positioning of an Object
$(\chi^2(1) = .600, p = .439)$.
Rotate
$(\chi^2(1) = .067, p = .796)$.

Table 10.4: Most likely expected actions for a control drag gesture

Results: The results show that the participants would most likely expect an action such as a 'Layout change', 'Rotation', or a 'Layout independent positioning of an Object' from the second multitouch gesture (Table 10.4). If we consider that 'Rotation' is a typical gesture to which multitouch device users are already familiar, than we can argue that the participants selecting 'Rotation' misunderstood the picture showing the gesture.

Nevertheless, we can say that the participants did significantly not expected the actions 'Zoom', 'Context', 'Change the position of the view camera', 'Show detail view', 'Show evolutionary view' for this gesture (Table 10.5).

Conclusion: For MQ2, we have to say that there is no significantly clear user expected action. However, the participants most likely expected to see a layout change. Showing a menu as suggested in our initial expectations allows a user to change the layout as well as other settings. A menu as a result to the second multitouch gesture can therefore still be considered an accurate action.

Show evolutionary view $(\chi^2(1) = 14.000, p < .001)$.
Zoom $(\chi^2(1) = 8.067, p < .01)$.
Show detail view $(\chi^2(1) = 8.067, p < .01)$.
Context $(\chi^2(1) = 5.4, p < .05)$.
Change the position of the view camera $(\chi^2(1) = 5.400, p < .05)$.

Table 10.5: Significant not expected actions for a control drag gesture

10.1.3 MQ3: Pinch gesture

MQ3 showed a gesture normally referred to as a pinch gesture, where two fingers are moved towards or apart from each other (Figure 10.3). The pinch gesture is a standard gesture used in several other graphic related multitouch applications. It is commonly used to zoom in an out of a view. We therefore expected a clear result for this gesture towards a 'Zoom' action.

Zoom $(\chi^2(1) = 15.0, p < .001)$.

Table 10.6: Significantly expected action for a pinch gesture

Calculation: The answers were again normalized into two categories and tested for significant answers with chi-square tests.

Results: The results for a pinch gesture showed a significantly clear expectation towards a 'Zoom' action. On the one hand significantly more participants answered, that the 'Zoom' action is appropriate for a pinch gesture (Table 10.6), and on the other hand significantly more participants expected the others actions are not appropriate for the pinch gesture (Table 10.7).

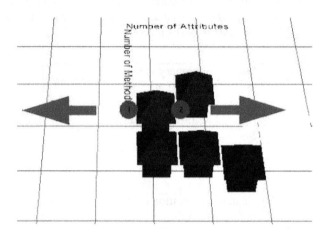

Figure 10.3: View presented in MQ3

Conclusion: We therefore can state that users expect a 'Zoom' action out of a pinch gesture when used in a graphical software exploration context.

Rotate
$(\chi^2(1) = 11.267, p < .001)$.
Context
$(\chi^2(1) = 14.0, p < .001)$.
Layout change
$(\chi^2(1) = 11.267, p < .001)$.
Show evolutionary view
$(\chi^2(1) = 14.000, p < .001)$.
Layout independent positioning of an Object
$(\chi^2(1) = 15.000, p < .001)$.
Change the position of the view camera
$(\chi^2(1) = 5.400, p < .05)$.

Table 10.7: Significantly not expected action for a pinch gesture

10.1.4 MQ4: Three touch move gesture

In MQ4, we showed a gesture, where an entity gets moved with three fingers (Figure 10.4). In Section 6.3.4 we referred to it as a three touch move gesture. The interaction of this gesture is intended to garb an entity with two more fingers and to move it around. However, the gesture is not typical and we have not experienced any similar gestures in other multitouch applications. We were not sure, on whether users would expect a 'Layout independent positioning of an Object' as a result to such a gesture.

Calculation: As in the previously multitouch questions, we tested for significant answers with chi-square tests after normalizing the answers into two categories.

Zoom $(\chi^2(1) = 7.143, p < .01)$.
Show evolutionary view $(\chi^2(1) = 7.143, p < .01)$.
Rotate $(\chi^2(1) = 6.231, p < .05)$.
Context $(\chi^2(1) = 5.333, p < .05)$.
Show detail view $(\chi^2(1) = 4.571, p < .05)$.

Table 10.8: Not expected action for a three touch move gesture

Results: The result for MQ4 were not significant for a single gesture. Still, the results showed that they were not expecting a 'Zoom', 'Rotate', 'Context', 'Show detail view', and 'Show evolutionary view' as an action to this gestures (Table 10.8).
Conclusion: For MQ4 we can state, that there is no significant expected action for participants. However, an action related to 'Layout independent positioning of an Object' is a feasible actions for this gesture.

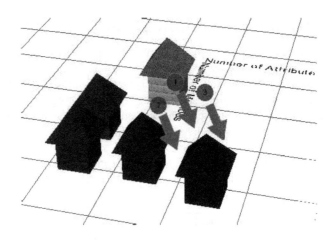

Figure 10.4: View presented in MQ4

10.1.5   MQ5: Swipe gesture

MQ5 showed a gesture were two fingers are moved fast to the left. In Section 6.3.3 we referred to it as a swipe gesture (Figure 10.5). The gesture is known from various other multitouch applications, but has no clear meaning such as for example a pinch gesture. In the software exploration context, we intended to map it to some action with regard to the selected entities. The idea was to trigger a evolutionary change view.

Calculation: As in the previously multitouch questions, a chi-square test was performed after normalizing the answers into two categories.

Results: The results for MQ5 were diverse and showed no significance towards an action. However, significantly more participants would not expect a 'Zoom', 'Rotate', 'Context', 'Layout change', or 'Show detail view' action as a result to that gesture (Table 10.9). Most likely the participants expected an action with regard to 'Show evolutionary view' or 'Change the position of the view camera'. If we consider the similarities of the dual-touch move gesture shown in the first multitouch question to the swipe gesture shown in the fifth multitouch question, we see that they distinguish themselves only by the speed of the gesture. We therefore can argue that some participants might have misinterpreted the picture shown with this gesture as equal to the first multitouch gesture and therefore chosen the 'Change the position of the view camera' action.

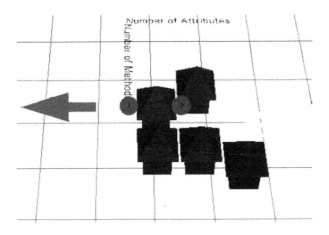

Figure 10.5: View presented in MQ5

Conclusion: For MQ5 we have to state that there is no significant clear action. Still, our intended 'Show evolutionary view' action is an aceptable action for the swipe gesture.

Zoom
$(\chi^2(1) = 14.000, p < .001)$.
Rotate
$(\chi^2(1) = 10.286, p < .001)$.
Context
$(\chi^2(1) = 4.571, p < .01)$.
Show detail view
$(\chi^2(1) = 9.308, p < .01)$.
Layout change
$(\chi^2(1) = 4.571, p < .05)$.

Table 10.9: Not expected gestures for a swipe gesture

10.1.6 MQ6: Wave path gesture

MQ6 showed a gesture with one finger moving to the right on a wave path (Figure 10.6). The gesture is not commonly known from other multitouch applications. In our software exploration context, we expected to map it to an action with regard to the selected entities. The idea was that while a swipe to the left would expect a evolutionary change a wave gesture to the right (or a swipe gesture to the right) would trigger a detailed view.

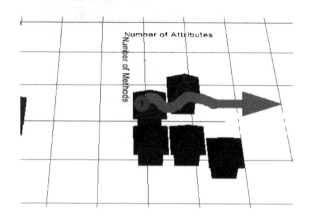

Figure 10.6: View presented in MQ6

Calculation: We used again a chi-square test after normalizing the answers into two categories.

Results: The results for MQ6 showed that the participants partially followed our expectations. There was no clear significance towards an action attributed to this gesture. However, the results showed significantly that they would not expect a 'Zoom', 'Rotate', 'Context', or 'Change the position of the view camera'.

Conclusion: We have to say that there is no significant clear action expected for a wave gesture. However an action with regard to a selected entity such as a evolutionary view or a detailed view is a feasible action for this gesture.

Zoom $(\chi^2(1) = 12.000, p < .001)$.
Rotate $(\chi^2(1) = 8.333, p < .01)$.
Context $(\chi^2(1) = 7.364, p < .01)$.
Change the position of the view camera $(\chi^2(1) = 8.333, p < .01)$.

Table 10.10: Significantly not expected action for a wave gesture

10.1.7 Résumé for the multitouch questions

We asked our participants to attribute their expected actions to a multitouch gesture. We showed that multitouch gestures familiar from other multitouch applications get the same expected action in our software visualization context. Furthermore we showed that unfamiliar gestures still get a clear direction to what kind of actions users expect. All our participants were unexperienced with our multitouch approach, and we still were able to show that their expectations were in line with our intended gesture mappings.

With regard to our Hypothesis 3b, we can say that an adequate mapping of actions to multitouch gestures allows us an intuitive exploration with almost no introduction of overhead.

Furthermore, in this survey we used all the actions necessary to explore a software project with our methodology. With our methodology we can solve most common software exploration issues. We therefore, consider our methodology a legitimate approach for software exploration. We mapped all the necessary actions used in our methodology to representative multitouch gestures. The results showed, that we were able to adequately map all actions needed for navigation and interaction in a software exploration context to specific multitouch gestures.

With regard to our Hypothesis 3a, we therefore can say that software exploration is adequately enabled on a multitouch screen with gestures mapped to navigation and interaction.

10.2 Results for the Aural Approach

With the result from our survey with regard to our aural approach we expect to verify that audio indeed supports a software exploration. In this section we intend to verify our Hypothesis 2a, Hypothesis 2b, and Hypothesis 2c (Section 1.3). In Hypothesis 2a we state that software metrics mapped to the pitch and tune of a sound sample permits an accurate categorization of the underlying software entity. Hypothesis 2b is the one, where we look, whether software metrics mapped to the pitch and tune of a sound sample permits an accurate perception of the evolutionary changes in the underlying software entity. Hypothesis 2c focuses on the opportunity to guide an observer in a three dimensional visualization to a specific position with the help of surround sounds. In the following, we present the results from our aural approach related survey questions.

10.2.1 AQ1: Sound-sample for potential errors in the code

In AQ1 we played a sound-sample of a boiling water. In Section 4.4 we referred to it as a intense and active sound. We expected users to feel this tension, that something is not calm and might have errors.

For the audio questions we used sixteen adjectives and their opposites (Table 10.11). We asked the participants to rate for each adjective according to their perception of the sound sample on a scale from one to nine. One meant the perceived sound sample adhered to the addictive, where as nine meant it adhered more to the opposite. The participants had also the choice to selected the option 'I do not know'.

Calculation: We took the answers for each adjective couple and categorized them on a nominal scale. All answer from one to four build a first category and the answer from six to nine build a second category. We than use chi-square tests, to verify the data for significant results.

Results: The results showed that significantly more participants answered, that the intense boiling water sound is an appropriate metaphor for software characteristics such as 'Error affected', 'Many changes', and 'Bad design' (Table 10.12).

Conclusion: We therefore can say that the participants sensed the tension in the boiling water as expected. They were also able to sense something big, more experimental, agile, with several changes, a worse design, and errors in the sound of boiling water.

Simple	Complex
Small	Large
Interesting	Not interesting
Calm	Active
Experimental	Stable
Imaginative	Neutral
Error afflicted	Flawless
Autonomous	Dependent
Robust	Weak
Bad designed	Well designed
Many lines of code	Few lines of code
Many methods	Few methods
Is not a class	Is a class
Is not a method	Is a method
Many changes	Few changes
Old component	New component

Table 10.11: Characteristics the participants described their audio perception

Experimental $(\chi^2(1) = 11.267, p < .001)$.
Active $(\chi^2(1) = 12.250, p < .001)$.
Many lines of code $(\chi^2(1) = 8.333, p < .01)$.
Bad design $(\chi^2(1) = 7.143, p < .01)$.
Imaginative $(\chi^2(1) = 9.308, p < .01)$.
Error afflicted $(\chi^2(1) = 9.308, p < .01)$.
Many changes $(\chi^2(1) = 7.364, p < .01)$.

Table 10.12: Significantly described adjectives for the sound of boiling water

10.2.2 AQ2: Sound-sample for potential error-free code

In AQ2, we played a sound-sample of a calm river like water flow. In Section 4.4 we referred to it as a calm and not intense sound. We expected users to feel fewer concerns in that part of the source code. The sample is considered the opposite of the sample used in the AQ1.

Calculation: Like in AQ1, we again categorized the answer for each adjective pair to a nominal scale and used a chi-square test to detect significant results.

Results: For the calm water significantly more participants answered that the calm water sound is an appropriate metaphor for software characteristics such as 'Small', 'Stable', and 'Few lines of code' (Table 10.13).

Small $(\chi^2(1) = 10.286, p < .001)$.
Neutral $(\chi^2(1) = 10.286, p < .001)$.
Stable $(\chi^2(1) = 7.143, p < .01)$.
Few lines of code $(\chi^2(1) = 6.231, p < .05)$.
Few methods $(\chi^2(1) = 6.400, p < .05)$.
Few changes $(\chi^2(1) = 4.455, p < .05)$.
Calm $(\chi^2(1) = 5.400, p < .05)$.

Table 10.13: Significantly described adjectives for the sound of calm water

Conclusion: We therefore can say that the calm water metaphor is sensed as expected. The users are able to sense something small, with fewer lines, less experimental and imaginative with few changes out of a calm water like sound sample. Combining the results from AQ1 and AQ2, we can state, that the water metaphor is adequate to distinguish lines of code, code structures, and code changes.

10.2.3 AQ3: Sound-sample for existing bugs in the code

In AQ3, we played a sound-sample of a sparkling water. In Section 4.4 we referred to it as a less intense and less active sound than the boiling water sample used in AQ1. We expected users to feel a little tension. We also expected them to feel that something might not be right and some errors exist in the source code. This example is intended to represent the intermediate situation between the sample used in the first aural question and the sample used in the second aural question. We presented the same sixteen adjectives and their opposites, used in the previous two question. Because of the adjectives representing extreme opposites, we did not expected any significances towards any adjective for this intermediate situation.

Calculation: We took the answers for each adjective couple and categorized them on a nominal scale. The first category combined the answer from one to four and the second category the answer from six to nine. With chi-square tests, we verify significant results. Beyond the categorization towards the extreme sides, for this intermediate situation we also checked for significances towards the middle values. For this situation we combined the answers from four to six together to a first category and the answers one to three and seven to nine to a second category. We used chi-square tests on the normalized categories with the weights set to 33% for category 1 and 66% for category 2, to verify the answers for significant results.

Results: The chi-square test for answers towards an extreme sides of an adjective, showed only one adjective significantly described by the sound sample. The participants found that the sound sample of sparkling water significantly describes only the adjective 'Faultier' in regards to a software entity (Table 10.14). The results for our tests towards middle values showed no significances at all.

Conclusion: We therefore can argue that the played sound of sparkling water is not interpreted as being exactly a middle situation between the sound sample played in AQ1 and the sound sample played in AQ2. The participants therefore independently experienced the sound sample describing the adjectives anywhere in between the two extremes values. The sound sample only decribed the software entity as 'Faultier' for a majority of participants.

Error afflicted
$(\chi^2(1) = 8.067, p < 0.01)$.

Table 10.14: Characteristic significantly describing the sound of sparkling water

10.2.4   AQ4: Alternative artificial sound-sample for AQ1

In AQ4, we played a sound-sample of a stressing electrical tone. The sound sample was used as a control question against the previous aural questions using the water metaphor. We expected users to feel that something is not calm and might have errors, a similar tension as they felt with the water metaphor but with a completely other metaphor. The difference however, is that this stressing electrical tone is artificial. For this sound sample there is no real cognitive known sound from our daily life.

Calculation: For the calculation we took the same adjective couple and categorized the answers again on a nominal scale. The first category with answers from one to four and the second one with answer from six to nine. With chi-square tests, we verified the answers for significances.

Results: The results were astonishing for us, because no-one of the adjective couple was found significantly more appropriate to describe the sample. Worse the answers were all spread along the nominal scale. The adjective with the highest tendency towards significancy, were 'Less imaginative' and 'Faultier' (Table 10.15).

Conclusion: We argue that the results for the artificial sound sample support our theory of how important the cognition of a used metaphor is. Our artificial sound sample does not represent any cognition. It is less imaginative and therefore can not be used to describe any entity characteristics.

Error afflicted
$(\chi^2(1) = 3.769, p = .052)$.
Neutral
$(\chi^2(1) = 2.250, p = .134)$.

Table 10.15: Characteristics with the highest tendency to describe an artificial sound

10.2.5 AQ5: Alternative cognitive sound-sample for AQ1

AQ5 similar as AQ4 is intended to serve as a control question against the aural questions using the water metaphor. In this question, we used a different non artificial metaphor cognitively known to the participants. We used a sound-sample of a starting motor engine with quite impulsive noise going up and downs. We wanted to see how different another cognitive known metaphor than the artificial or the water metaphor would perform. Because of its cognitive meaning, we expected more significant results than for the artificial tone used in the fourth aural question. However, the sound of a motor engine is quite special. It has several characteristics that are hard to percept. We expected the sound sample appropriately describing fewer adjectives than with the water metaphor.

Calculation: The answers were normalized the same way as in the previous aural questions and we used again chi-square tests to verify the data for significant results.

Results: The results showed that significantly more participants found the motor engine characterizing a complex, agile and older software component (Table 10.16).

Complex $(\chi^2(1) = 8.067, p < .01)$.
Old component $(\chi^2(1) = 4.500, p < .05)$.
Active $(\chi^2(1) = 5.333, p < .05)$.

Table 10.16: Adjective with the highest tendency to describe our artificial sound

Conclusion: With these results our argumentation from the previous aural questions remains the same. It is important for a sound sample how understandable the cognitive metaphor is. While the artificial sound sample used in AQ4 did not represent any cognitive meaning. In the case of the motor engine a cognitive meaning is present. Still, the sound sample is complex and therefore it is as well hard to characterize a software component with that metaphor.

10.2.6   AQ6: Decreasing evolutionary growth changes in code

In AQ6, we focused on the coding of evolutionary information into aural feedback. The idea is to percept a evolutionary change of a software entity as a change of a sound characteristics. Our evolutionary sound-sample showed four tones played in a sequence. In the sound-sample used in AQ6 each tone is lower than the previous tone. The tones are played with a bass instrument. From this sound-sample we expected participants to feel a software entity become smaller over time.

Calculation: For the evolutionary aural feedback, we used the same adjective couples used before (Table 10.17). To assemble the answers for the evolutionary aural feedback, we categorized them into two categories in the same was in the previous aural questions. The chi-square tests was used to validate significant answers.

Simple	Complex
Small	Large
Interesting	Not interesting
Autonomous	Dependent
Resistant	Weak
Grew at the beginning	Decreased at the beginning
Grew over the time	Decreased over the time
Grew at the end	Decreased at the end
Few changes	Many changes
Negative changes	Positive changes
Bad designed	Well designed
Many lines of code	Few lines of code
Error afflicted	Flawless
Old component	New component
Was changed	Was not changed
Was improved	Was not improved

Table 10.17: Characteristics the participants could describe the evolutionary audio perception

Results: The answers of our participants significantly showed that they felt the aural feedback in AQ6 describing a small, simple, and older software entity. The evolutionary aural feedback further described an entity with few changes, that decreased over time and in particular decreased during the last iteration (Table 10.18).

Simple $(\chi^2(1) = 7.143, p < .01)$.
Small $(\chi^2(1) = 9.308, p < .01)$.
Few lines of code $(\chi^2(1) = 8.000, p < .01)$.
Decreased over time $(\chi^2(1) = 6.400, p < .05)$.
Decreased at the end $(\chi^2(1) = 5.444, p < .05)$.
Few changes $(\chi^2(1) = 5.400, p < .05)$.
Old component $(\chi^2(1) = 3.600, p = .058)$.

Table 10.18: Significantly described adjective for AQ6

The results for the AQ6, were four tones are played each one lower than the one before, covers almost our expectations. We see, that significantly more participants interpreted the tones getting lower and lower as a software entities becoming smaller over time. However, we noticed that the participants did not interpreted the first lower sound interval as a software entity becoming smaller. This even though the second tone was notably lower than the first tone. On the other side significantly more participants found the sound sequence would suggest a decreasing of the described software entity over time. Our argumentation is that they probably needed at least one sound interval to feel a change at all. For the significant interpretations of the 'Simple', 'Small', and 'Few lines of code' our argument is, that the participants most likely sensed the four really low tones of a bass instrument particularly small, simple. A total lower pitch of the sound sequence, also suggests a simpler and smaller software entity.

Conclusion: For AQ6, we state that a low total pitch of a tone suggests a simple and smaller size. We further see that an aural sequence, where the tones gets lower over time really can be used to represent negative software changes over time.

10.2.7 AQ7: Stagnating evolutionary growth changes in code

With AQ7, we wanted to see how the participants experience changes in time, that do not really result in any grown entities. The representing aural feedback played four sequentially tones, where the first two tones played downwards interval and the second two tones upward intervals back to the starting tone. We used the same low bass instrument as in AQ6 to play the tones. Our expectation is that the participants feel a software entity that has gone under changes over time.

Calculation: Calculations were done the same way as before. We categorized the questions to two categories and used chi-square tests.

Results: The results showed that participants described the evolutionary aural feedback as representative for a small, rather interesting software entity with few lines of code and a bad design (Table 10.19).

Small $(\chi^2(1) = 10.000, p < .01)$.
Few lines of code $(\chi^2(1) = 4.500, p < .05)$.
Interesting $(\chi^2(1) = 3.769, p = .052)$.
Bad desiged $(\chi^2(1) = 3.600, p = .058)$.

Table 10.19: Significantly described adjective for AQ7

In the results, we see that the participants did experienced changes and an entity that did not just got smaller compared to what they saw in AQ6. They still interpret the software entity as a small component with few lines of code. A majority of the participants saw the aural feedback representing a software entity that is rather interesting but interpreted its design as bad.

Conclusion: For AQ7, we can say that again, a low total pitch of a tone suggests a smaller entity with few lines. We further see that an aural sequence with bidirectional changes, provoked more interest toward the entity and more concerns about the design.

10.2.8 AQ8: Increasing evolutionary growth changes in code

AQ8 is considered the opposite of AQ6. We wanted to see how the participants experience a software entity that normally growths over time. The played aural feedback consisted of four tones, where each one is higher than the one before. The tones were played with a low bass instrument.

Calculation: As before the answers for this question were normalized to two categories. Significant answers were evaluated with chi-square tests.

Results: The results showed more participants answered the aural feedback representing a simple, small software entity with few lines of codes. According to the participants the represented software entity has grown over time and had changes since the last release (Table 10.20).

Small $(\chi^2(1) = 11.000, p < .001)$.
Few lines of code $(\chi^2(1) = 9.000, p < .01)$.
Simple $(\chi^2(1) = 5.333, p < .05)$.
Grown over time $(\chi^2(1) = 5.444, p < .05)$.
Grown at the end $(\chi^2(1) = 4.500, p < .05)$.

Table 10.20: Significantly described adjective for AQ8

The results for the use case were the four tones played each one is higher than the one before are in line with our expectations. Significantly more participants interpreted the higher tones as software entities that grows over time. A majority of the participants interpreted the last higher interval as well as an entity that grew at the end of the software evolution. The other significant answers are in line with what we already saw in AQ6 and AQ7. The participants most likely sensed the four low tone of a bass instrument as a small software entity with few lines of code, and the four normal ascending tones as simple changes to the entity.

Conclusion: In AQ8, we see again, that low total pitch of a tone suggests a smaller entity with few lines. We also see that an aural sequence that is constantly growing, really was interpreted as a growing software component.

10.2.9 AQ9: Mixed evolutionary growth changes

With AQ9 we wanted to investigate how participants experience changes in time that increased and eventually a reengineering brought them down again. For the aural feedback we used four tones, where the first two played upward intervals and the second two downward intervals. The sequence ended on a lower level than the starting point. To play the sequence we used the same low bass instrument. Our expectations were that participants felt a software entity that grew and went under reengineering changes end the end.

Calculation: We used the same normalization into two categories as before and analyzed for significant answers with chi-square tests.

Results: The results showed significantly more participants experienced an older, faulty software component with bad designed and resent changes. A majority of the participants also experienced a weak, dependent component (Table 10.21).

Worse design
$(\chi^2(1) = 6.400, p < .05)$.
Error afflicted
$(\chi^2(1) = 6.400 p < .05)$.
Old component
$(\chi^2(1) = 5.444, p < .05)$.
Decreased at the end
$(\chi^2(1) = 4.00, p < .05)$.
Weak
$(\chi^2(1) = 3.600, p = .058)$.
Dependent
$(\chi^2(1) = 3.571, p = .059)$.

Table 10.21: Significantly described adjective for AQ9

The results for AQ9 showed some interesting results. As expected significantly more participants interpreted the downward interval at the end as a software entities that got smaller at the end. A majority of participants also interpreted the sequence going up and down as a faulty, old software component with a bad design. We think that this is because of the special situation of a growing software entity that suddenly drops in size. Such a situation typically arise during reengineering processes or bugfixes. Our argumentation is further supported by a majority of the participants interpreting the component as dependent and weak. Two other adjectives that can be considered describing a faulty and error prone software.

Conclusion: We therefore can conclude that a evolutionary aural feedback can be used to perceive changes in size over time.

10.2.10 AQ10: Guiding an observer with ambient audio

With AQ10 we focused on our ambient audio approach. The goal was to show, that in a three dimensional visualization in using surround sound technology, we can guide an observer to a specific position. For the experiment we created four sound samples from different places in the visualization (Figure 10.7). For the sound samples, we used the water metaphor effectively used in the previous aural questions. The participants were presented a software visualization were we marked the positions from which we recorded the sound samples. They were able to listen to the four sound sample independently. We gave the participants the assignment to look for entities with a lot of changes in the past. Based on the heard sample, they had to answer, towards which marked position they would move the marker. We expected the users to move towards position one as the sound sample there was boiling the most.

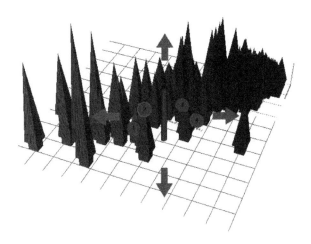

Figure 10.7: View presented to AQ10 and AQ11

Calculation: For the calculation we categorized the answers on a nominal scale. In this use case the first category represented all the answer for participants moving to our expected position one. In the second category we combined the answers for the other three positions in the presented software visualization (Figure 10.7). We used chi-square tests, were the weights where set to 25% for the first category and 75% for the second category to verified the data for significant results.

Results: The results showed that in our experiment indeed highly significant more participants moved their attention towards the expected position one (Table 10.22).

Choose to move to expected point 1
$(\chi^2(1) = 18.689, p < .001)$.

Table 10.22: Significant more participants were guided to point 1 in AQ10

Conclusion: We therefore can conclude, that ambient audio is understood as intended and can be used as a way to guide observers to entities with a lot of changes in the past.

10.2.11 AQ11: Ambient audio control question

AQ11 is considered a control question to AQ10. The set up is almost the same, in that we created four ambient audio sample based on the water metaphor. In the same way, we presented our participant a visualization, were we marked the positions, from were the sound samples were created. This time, we asked the users, were they would expect the least bug prone software components. Our expectation was that users would chose position two in the visualization, as in position two the calmest sound sample was played (Figure 10.7).

Choose to move to expected point 2
$(\chi^2(1) = 13.889, p < .001)$.

Table 10.23: Significant more participants were guided to point 2 in AQ11

Calculation: The calculations were the same as in AQ10. Only this time the first category represented all the answer for participants moving to our expected position two. In the second category, we combined all the answers for the other three categories. To verified the answers for significant results, we again used chi-square tests, with the weights where set to 25% for the first category and 75% for the second category.

Results: The results of our chi-square tests, showed that highly significant more participants would move towards the expected position two (Table 10.23).

Conclusion: For AQ11 we therefore can say, that in a three dimensional visualization with the use of surround sound technology and adequate sound metaphor, we can guide an observer to a specific position.

10.2.12 Résumé for the aural questions

We asked unexperienced participants to listen to sound samples and attribute their perceived feelings towards a software component represented by that particular sound sample. We were able to show, that using an adequate sound metaphor such as the water metaphor enables users to adequately distinguish characteristics of software components such as lines of code, code structures and changes (AQ1-AQ3). With the use of artificial tones not representing any familiar cognitive meaning (AQ4 and AQ5), we were furthermore able to show that the lake of a cognitive meaning, also affects the ability of adequately distinguish software characteristics. With that we were able to show, how important an understandable cognitive metaphor for such a purpose is.

With regard to our Hypothesis 2a we therefore can say, that software metrics mapped to the pitch and tune of a sound sample indeed permit an accurate categorization of the underlying software entity.

Concerning our evolutionary aural feedback (AQ6-AQ9), we can state that significantly more participants accurately interpreted changes in size over time and were able to feel weak, faulty, dependent and old software components with bad designs.

With regard to our Hypothesis 2b, we can therefore conclude, that software metrics mapped to the pitch and tune of a sound sample also permit an accurate perception of the evolutionary changes in the underlying software entity.

With regard to our ambient audio approach (AQ10 and AQ11), we were able to show, that highly significant more participants were moving their attention to the expected positions.

For our Hypothesis 2c, we therefore can conclude that surround sound technology combined with an adequate sound metaphor, are suitable to guide an observer to a specific position in a 3D visualization.

We showed that surround sound techniques can adequately guide an observer in a 3D visualization. Other scientific work, showed that force directed graphs can be used in software visualization to layout software entities based on their interconnectivity [FPG03].

In combining these results and using stability metrics such as number of bug reports to create our aural feedback, we are able to guide users in a software visualization, while perceiving the stability of the interconnected software entities. With this combination, we can further accept our Hypothesis 2d.

10.3 Results for the Visual Approach

With the results with regard to our visual approach, we expect to verify that cognitive knowledge indeed can be used to support a software exploration. We intend to verify our Hypothesis 1a (Section 1.3), where we state that software metrics mapped to object known from our daily lives permit an effective categorization of the underlying software entity. Furthermore we verify Hypothesis 1b (Section 1.3), where we state that software metrics mapped to the width and length of an object known from our daily lives allow a comparison of the underlying software entity.

We specified four survey questions with regard to the visual approach. With the first three visual questions, we wanted to see how participants experience cognitive objects and what adjectives and measurements interpret the shown cognitive objects best. We used fifteen adjectives and their opposites to describe the participants interpretation (Table 10.24). The participants were asked to rate according to their interpretation of the cognitive object for each of the fifteen adjectives on a scale from one to nine. One meant the cognitive objects adhered to the addictive, where as nine meant it adhered more to the opposite. The participants had also the choice to selected the option 'I do not know'.

Simple	Complex
Small	Large
Interesting	Not interesting
Imaginative	Neutral
Experimental	Stable
Autonomous	Dependent
Robust	Weak
Few lines of code	Many lines of code
Few methods	Many methods
Is a class	Is not a class
Is a method	Is not a method
Error afflicted	Flawless
Old component	New component
Few changes	Several changes
Bad designed	Well designed

Table 10.24: Characteristics the participants could describe the visual objects

In the four questions with regard to the visual approach, we compared our approach to other ones. We wanted to see, whether some adjectives are better perceived with our cognitive metaphor approach in comparison to other approaches.

In the following, we present the results from our survey questions related to the visual approach.

10.3.1 VQ1: Well-formed house

For VQ1, we used a simple object from our house metaphor. The presented object represented a house with a well-formed roof and body (Figure 10.8). Our expectation was, that participants felt a stable software entity with few open issues.

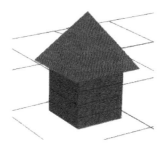

Figure 10.8: Object presented in VQ1

Calculation: To test the participants answers for significant relations, we took the answers for each adjective or measurements and categorized them on a nominal scale. All answer from one to four built a first category and the answer from six to nine built a second category. We used chi-square tests to verify the data for significant results.

Results: The results for VQ1 showed some expected and interesting outcomes (Table 10.25). As expected significantly more participants interpreted the first object representing a stable neutral software entity. They also significantly expected an older component, with fewer recent changes. We think that this is due to the size the object represented compared to other similar objects. Interesting for the house metaphor in general are the result that the participants significantly did not expected the object to represent a method. They more likely expect the object to represent a class.

Simple $(\chi^2(1) = 12.000, p < .001)$.
Stable $(\chi^2(1) = 12.000, p < .001)$.
Neutral $(\chi^2(1) = 13.000, p < .001)$.
Is not a method $(\chi^2(1) = 9.000, p < .01)$.
Old component $(\chi^2(1) = 7.000, p < .01)$.
Few changes $(\chi^2(1) = 7.000, p < .01)$.
Is a class $(\chi^2(1) = 2.778, p = .096)$.

Table 10.25: Characteristics used to describe the visual object in VQ1

Conclusion: We can state that for a simple well-shaped house object (Figure 10.8), as expected significantly more participants interpret a stable software entity with few changes.

10.3.2 VQ2: Small not well-shaped house

In VQ2, we used a smaller and not well-shaped object from our house metaphor. The roof of the house is smaller than the body what results in a non typical house metaphor (Figure 10.9). Our expectations were that participants felt a not so stable smaller software entity with some open issues.

Calculation: In the same way as in VQ1, the answers were normalized into two categories. To verify for significant results, we applied chi-square tests on the categorized dataset.

Results: In the results, we see that significantly more participants see the object in VQ2 representing a smaller, simple software object with few methods and lines of codes (Table 10.26). We think that the participants described this object with these characteristics due to the smaller size of the object shown in VQ2 compared to the one in VQ1. Interesting is further, that significantly more participants see the object worse designed than the one shown in VQ1. We explain this description as a result

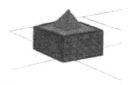

Figure 10.9: Object presented in VQ2

of the roof-body ratio of the second house object not representing a typical house.

Smaller $(\chi^2(1) = 8.333, p < .01)$.
Few lines of code $(\chi^2(1) = 10.000, p < .01)$.
Few methods $(\chi^2(1) = 10.000, p < .01)$.
Simple $(\chi^2(1) = 6.231, p < .05)$.
Bad designed $(\chi^2(1) = 5.333, p < .05)$.
Is not a method $(\chi^2(1) = 3.571, p = .059)$.

Table 10.26: Characteristics used to describe the visual object in VQ2

Conclusion: We can state that for a small not well-shaped house object with a roof smaller than the body (Figure 10.9), significantly more participants interpret a small software entity with a bad design.

10.3.3 VQ3: Miss-shaped house

In VQ3, we used a miss-shaped house object with a roof-body ratio inverse to the one used in VQ2. The difference is that the house object in VQ3 has a roof that is notably larger than normal compared to its body (Figure 10.10). Our expectations were that participants felt again a not so stable smaller software entity with some issues open.

Figure 10.10: Object presented in VQ3

Calculation: For VQ3, we used the same adjective couples used before (Table 10.24). We categorized them into two categories in the same was in the previous visual questions and used again chi-square tests to validate the dataset for significant answers.

Results: The results show that the participants see the visual object in VQ3 representing rather an older software component with few lines of code and a bad design (Table 10.27). Interesting in these results is, that the participants see the visual object in VQ3 representing a more stable and neutral software entity compared to the object shown in VQ2. Our explanation for this is, that even though the third visual object has a oversized roof and it is not well-shaped at all, it is better recognizable as a house. However, the visual object in VQ3 in general is not intended as good as the visual object shown in VQ1. The participants compare the visual object in VQ3 more with a less robust, weak, and bad designed software entity. The characteristic of a bad design most likely arises from the not typical roof-body ratio of the house in VQ3.

Conclusion: We can state that for a small miss-shaped house object with a roof bigger than the body, significantly more participants interpret a small, bad designed software entity. Furthermore we see, that the house metaphor is not intuitive enough to represent methods but the size of the houses is enough understandable to represent code size.

Is not a method $(\chi^2(1) = 7.000, p < .01)$.
Few lines of code $(\chi^2(1) = 5.333, p < .05)$.
Bad designed $(\chi^2(1) = 6.400, p < .05)$.
Old component $(\chi^2(1) = 4.500, p < .05)$.
Neutral $(\chi^2(1) = 4.455, p < .05)$.
Weak $(\chi^2(1) = 3.600, p = .058)$.
Stable $(\chi^2(1) = 3.600, p = .058)$.

Table 10.27: Characteristics used to describe the visual object in VQ3

10.3.4 VQ4: Visual comparison question

In VQ4, we compared our cognitive approach to a different one. In comparing our approach to a different one, we wanted to see whether some adjectives are better perceived with our cognitive metaphor approach. For that, we presented an entity from our visual approach together with the entity as visualized in the code city approach [WL08]. For comparison reason we used only similar visual objects and not the full visualizations of the different approaches. We used again our fifteen adjectives and their opposites to describe the participants interpretation (Table 10.24).

The participants were than asked to state, which adjective is more likely represented in our approach compared to the other approach. For each adjective, they had to answer on a scale from one to nine. One meant our approach compared to the other adhered rather to the shown addictive, where as nine meant it adhered more to the opposite. The participants had also the choice to selected the option 'I do not know'. For the question we used a simple object from our house metaphor together with its counterpart in code city (Figure 10.11). Our expectations were that participants would perceive the size and complexity of the software entity.

Calculation: In the same way as in the previous questions, we categorized the answers into two categories. All answers from one to four build a first category and

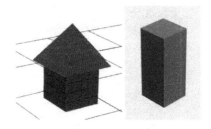

Figure 10.11: Objects presented in VQ4

the answer from six to nine build a second category. We then use chi-square tests, to verify the data for significant results.

Complexer $(\chi^2(1) = 8.333, p < .01)$.
Larger $(\chi^2(1) = 10.000, p < .01)$.
More methods $(\chi^2(1) = 8.000, p < .01)$.
More interesting $(\chi^2(1) = 7.364, p < .01)$.
More lines of code $(\chi^2(1) = 6.400, p < .05)$.
More Imaginative $(\chi^2(1) = 6.400, p < .05)$.
More Experimental $(\chi^2(1) = 3.600, p = .058)$.
More autonomous $(\chi^2(1) = 3.571, p = .059)$.

Table 10.28: Characteristics used to compare our visual approach to others

Results: The results show that significantly more participants understood our approach rather representative for software components with regard to characteristics such as 'Complexity', 'Size', and 'Lines of Code' (Table 10.28). With regard to the characteristics of 'More interesting' and 'Imaginative' significantly more participants adhere those to our house metaphor as well. We argue that this is most likely due to their cognition with regard to the house metaphor.

Conclusion: With the results of our comparison, we can state that with the house metaphor some software characteristics such as 'Complexity', 'Size' and 'Lines of codes' are perceived better compared to the code city approach.

10.3.5 Paired Samples Test

In this part, we want to test whether our cognitive metaphors allow for a comparison of the underlying software entity as stated in Hypothesis 1b (Section 1.3). For that, we used the answers our participants gave in the first three visual questions. We wanted to verify whether the answers our participants gave with regard to the different cognitive metaphors present in these three visual questions are indeed significantly different.

Calculation: To test the answers of the three visual questions for significant differences, we planed to use t-tests. The use of t-tests requires a dataset with a normal distribution. To assure our dataset meets the requirements, we using a Kolmogorov-Smirnov-Test. We tested the answers for each adjective in our dataset for a normal distribution on a confidence interval of 95 %. Our Kolmogorov-Smirnov-Tests showed that the answers in our dataset, are normal distribution on a confidence interval of 95 %, and eligible to use in a t-test. To calculate the differences between the three cognitive metaphors, we used a dependent t-test. We paired the answers of the related questions and calculated the t value from the mean of differences and the standard error of differences. As a confidence interval we used 95 %.

Results: The results showed that the participants significantly perceived the compared house metaphors (Figures 10.8, 10.9, 10.10) different with regard to eight characteristics (Table 10.29). Within the tested characteristics not all three compared objects are significantly different from each other. We argue that this is as well due to the participants not experiencing the differences equally extreme. In the following we try to explain some of the experienced differences.

With regard to 'Simpler' the participants saw the first software entity represented by a neutral well-shaped house significantly 'Simpler' than the third one with an over proportioned roof. The first visual object was however not experienced dif-

Simple
first visual object significantly not equal to the third visual object $(t(12) = 2.194, p < .05)$
Small
first visual object significantly not equal to the second visual object $(t(12) = 2.325, p < .05)$
Few methods
second visual object weakly not equal to the third visual object $(t(12) = -2144, p = .053)$
Bad designed
first visual object significantly not equal to the second visual object $(t(12) = 2.490, p < .05)$
Experimental
first visual object significantly not equal to the second visual object $(t(12) = 3.207, p < .01)$ second visual object significantly not equal to the third visual object $(t(12) = -2.843, p < .05)$
Imaginative
first visual object significantly not equal to the second visual object $(t(12) = 3.323, p < .01)$ second visual object significantly not equal to the third visual object $(t(12) = -2.770, p < .05)$
Error afflicted
first visual object significantly not equal to the second visual object $(t(12) = 3.323, p < .01)$ second visual object significantly not equal to the third visual object $(t(12) = -2.770, p < .05)$
Robust
first visual object weakly not equal to the second visual object $(t(12) = -2133, p = .054)$ first visual object significantly not equal to the third visual object $(t(12) = 2.499, p < .05)$

Table 10.29: Characteristics with significant differences between the visual objects used in VQ1,VQ2, and VQ3

ferent compared to the second visual object. A reason for this could be that the second visual object is smaller in size than the first one and the roof is smaller than the body but not enough to make a significant difference. We suspect that concerning 'Size' the participants perceived the first object clearly 'bigger' than the second one. Interestingly we see that when talking about 'Fewer methods', the participants distinguished the second object from the third one. The two objects distinguish themselves mainly in the roof size. The roof therefore seam to be a good place to map size metrics such as 'Number of Methods'. Concerning the design the participants distinguished the rather neutral first visual object from the second one with a smaller roof. Having a house body with an unnatural roof clearly seams to trigger the perception of a software entity with a bad design. With regard to the rather emotional questions about how experimental or imaginative a software entity represented by the visual object was perceived, all the three object were distinguished significantly different. In our argumentation this is a result of the cognitive behavior. Two other good characteristics to distinguish software entities with the house metaphor are found in how faulty or robust a software entity is. The participants were able to significantly distinguish all the three objects.

Conclusion: With the provided test, we could show that the house metaphor is suitable to compare the different software entities. With the performed test, we did not focus on how fine-graded the changes need to be. With regard to the level of granularity, we therefore argue that our software visualization is not intended to represent exact measurements rather than offer a basic distinction.

10.3.6 Résumé for the visual questions

We asked participants unfamiliar with our approach to attribute their perception towards a software component represented by a visual object from our house metaphor. From the given answers, we were able to show that the use of a house metaphor enables users to adequately distinguish characteristics of software components such size, complexity and bug metrics.

With regard to our Hypothesis 1a (Section 1.3), we therefore can say that software metrics mapped to object known from our daily lives permit an effective categorization of the underlying software entity.

With tests on whether the participants were able to distinguish characteristics among similar visual objects, we focused on the comparison of underlying software entities. We showed that participants indeed were able to significantly distinguish characteristics among similar objects.

With regard to our Hypothesis 1b, we can conclude that software metrics mapped to objects known from our daily lives allow for a comparison of the underlying software entity, even without knowledge of the underlying mapping.

10.4 Overall Résumé

In this chapter, we focused on the validations of our approach. We presented the results of our survey and tested them against the hypothesis of this thesis. We accessed the various areas of our thesis as independent as possible and combine the results to address the applicability of the overall approach for an efficient software visualization. In the following, we summarize the results.

- With regard to our Hypothesis 1a, we showed that software metrics mapped to objects known from our daily lives permit an effective categorization of the underlying software entity.

- With regard to our Hypothesis 1b, we concluded that software metrics mapped to objects known from our daily lives allow for a comparison of the underlying software entity, even without knowledge of the underlining mapping.

- With regard to our Hypothesis 2a we showed that software metrics mapped to the pitch and tune of a sound sample permit an accurate categorization of the underlying software entity.

- With regard to our Hypothesis 2b, we concluded that software metrics mapped to the pitch and tune of a sound sample also permit an accurate perception of the evolutionary changes in the underlying software entity.

- For our Hypothesis 2c, we concluded that surround sound technology combined with an adequate sound metaphor, are suitable to guide an observer to a specific position in a 3D visualization.

- For Hypothesis 2d, we showed that in combining the results of Hypothesis 2c with results from other researchers on force-directed layout algorithm, allows us an assessment of the stability of interconnected software entities.

- With regard to our Hypothesis 3a, we therefore can say that software exploration can be adequately enabled on a multitouch screen with gestures mapped to navigation and interaction.

- With regard to our Hypothesis 3b, we showed that an adequate mapping of actions to multitouch gestures allows us an intuitive exploration with almost no introduction of overhead.

Part IV
Retrospection

11
Contributions to Software Engineering

Software systems often grow into the many million lines of code, a size that can not been overlooked by a simple engineer anymore. Working on a project involving several groups brings in a dimension of complexity that becomes even harder to control over time. With the growing of a project, its performance, design and stability become more and more important factors for the success of the project. Among the goals of the software engineering research community are to develop tools and methodologies to simplify the development and maintenance of software projects.

Over the years the introduction of programming paradigms, design patterns, object oriented programming languages and capabilities of debugging source code as close as during runtime allowed to increase accuracy and stability. The toolsets became much more sophisticated, where modern integrated development environments support the development, with code completion, on the fly syntax checking and source code analysis.

Still evolving software brings in new challenges. Previous designs become obsolete and inefficient, inconsequent modifications affect stability and knowledge gets lost with leaving developers. Concerns in software evolution are part of the software engineering research. Results that benefit understanding software evolution therefore contribute to software engineering. With our approaches to support the perception of software and its evolution we directly addressed how to facilitate software understanding. Our research motivation was driven by materializing the abstract essence of software and concretize its understanding.

Osterweil in his work on the future of software engineering presented two research motivations [Ost07]. A problem-solving-oriented approach and a curiosity-driven research approach. During this dissertation we found ourselves often motivated to use new technologies and scientific results to address the understanding problems. We were rather curios in how to use technologies only few people have used in software engineering before and looked at how we could adapt solutions from other fields to benefit software development and maintenance. We found that playing with our curiosity led us to implement our approaches on optimized visual perception and the use of our other human senses.

All the approaches presented in COCOVIZ contribute to simplify the exploration and understanding of software evolution. In this chapter, we summarize our contribution to software evolution and maintenance.

11.1 Understanding Software Evolution

Several approaches of our thesis contribute to improve understandability of software evolution.

11.1.1 On the perception of software projects

Understanding software is achieved by reading the source code, relying on developers' comments and involving everyones own imagination of an abstract nature. Reading the source code however limits the understanding on a small specific part and developers tend to neglect how important it is to maintain existing information. Lakhotia sees possible reasons for this neglecting in deadline pressure and carelessness [Lak93].

Software visualization offers a different way to grasp a picture of the software system: In materializing the abstract essence of software with measured characteristics. The so called metrics allow one to look at a software from a dedicated point of view. Over the years several visualization approaches emerged with diverse focus.

We developed a software visualization approach, that not only visualizes software metrics but takes into account the cognitive knowledge of an observer. With so called cognitive glyphs, we are able to map metrics to characteristics of objects known from our daily lives (*e. g.* a simple house). The observer because of its cognitive knowledge about these objects can perceive the software characteristics more intuitively and without the need to know about the source code.

This approach allows exploration of a software for developers unfamiliar to the architecture, to receive an overview of relevant components. Furthermore it opens a discussion platform for involved parties such as management and project leaders not capable to understand source code. Our visual approach contributes to understanding software with its intuitive perception of present architecture, the involved software entities, structures and relations.

11.1.2 Access information without losing focus

Thinking of perceiving information, we found that most of the research in software visualization focuses only on the visual human sense. Especially in situations where a task needed further information, this was not easily accessible and in some cases required the creation of a different visualization. The creation of such a visualization would result in progressively losing the focus from the primary task. In reading Pacione's work on levels of abstraction in visualization for software comprehension, we thought about how to adequately access multiple of these abstraction levels [Pac04]. We came up with the idea to use aural notifications to inform an observer about secondary information. The idea was similar to a movie, where music and noise support the visual perception, we could map software metrics to sound samples.

With our entity audio we developed an approach to perceive secondary information about software entities over an aural feedback. An aural feedback is a sound sample where software metrics are mapped to the characteristics of the sound sample. The characteristics of a sound sample are the parameters that if changed, are distinguishable. According to Zwicker et al. such parameters are loudness, sharpness, tone pitch, roughness and oscillation [ZFH01].

The approach was further extended to allow a simple and intuitive exploration of software entities historical chances. This is achieved by creating the sound samples for the various releases and playing them as a sequence. Through this an observer can easily see whether a software entity was recently changed or how intense the software entity grew over time.

Our entity audio approach contributes to understanding software with its intuitive perception of secondary information and simple exploration of historical changes.

11.1.3 Intuitive interaction for software exploration

Looking at use cases where our cognitive software visualization would fit in a typical development and maintenance workflow, we picked a common software review where engineers, project leaders and management would sit together and discuss future plans.

With common beamer or monitor techniques the exploration of the software system would be limited to the person with the controller. According to Hilliges *et al.* a classical single- user system in a collaborative setting leads in most cases to a communication breakdown since the user's concentration has to shift away from the group and towards the computer in order to use it [HTB+07].

The use of multitouch-tables shows a more intuitive and natural interaction with the software visualization, brings the involved parties closer together on a table and further supports collaboration.

With our tactile approach we developed a framework to map gestures to intuitive software exploration interactions. Our studies showed that an intuitive mapping on top of its natural behavior, further simplifies the software exploration with a fast and easy learning process.

Our tactile approach contributes to understanding software exploration with its intuitive and natural interaction accessible by multiple engineers and enforcing a face to face discussion.

11.2 Supporting Software Exploration

The several approaches of our thesis contribute to supporting software exploration pertaining to the following perspectives.

11.2.1 An approach to guide observers to relevant aspects

When we implemented the entity audio approach we thought about what information is passed to the observer with an aural feedback. We found it disturbing that when multiple potential solutions were visualized we had to click independently on each of them to perceive the secondary information.

We wanted to get rid of these independent clicks and came up with the idea that the entities should tell us which ones are more important in regards to the actual focus. With ambient audio we implemented an approach where the entities get a combined aural feedback based on its position in the visualization and its importance to the actual point of discussion. For the aural feedback we used sound samples allowing to change the feedback characteristics with the Zwicker parameters [ZFH01]. We then used surround sound technologies to allocate the sound samples to the visual objects position. With this approach an observer can now move around the software visualization and listen to the aural feedback at that location. This allows an observer to perceive directions and navigate directly to the points of interest.

Our ambient audio approach contributes to supporting software exploration with a new and intuitive way to guide an observer to the points of interest in showing an acoustic navigation path.

11.2.2 A simplified configuration of common tasks

When looking at the creation of a software visualization, we noticed that most of the time a profound knowledge about the configuration was needed. Especially if an engineer looked for an adequate configuration for a common comprehension task. Such a configuration effort could prevent engineers from using software visualization. Our effort brought us to simplify the configuration effort at least for most common comprehension tasks.

With our automated comprehension tasks, we developed a framework to create presets of adequate software visualizations for common comprehension task. The presets are composed of automated configuration and macro steps. Through such automated tasks we are able to lower the effort for an engineer to access an adequate software visualization to a minimum for most common comprehension tasks.

Our approach on automated tasks contributes to supporting software exploration in lowering the configuration threshold to access an adequate software visualization.

11.3 Résumé

Exploring the evolution of software is a research direction of software engineering. In our dissertation we addressed the research field regarding to software exploration and understanding software evolution. We therefore contributed to software engineering pertaining to the following perspectives:

- understanding software evolution by investigating the nature of software perception with our human senses;

- supporting software exploration by simplifying the configuration process to access software visualization and in guiding the observer to relevant aspects.

In this thesis, we showed that the use of cognitive comprehensive software visualization, supported with aural feedback and a tactile interaction contributes to the understanding of software evolution and to the support of software exploration.

Part V

Closing

12

Conclusion

Software visualization is an effective way to better understand a software project. With COCOVIZ we presented an approach that enriches software visualization and its perception with the use of our various senses. In using the cognitive knowledge of individuals we were able to improve perception and distinction of software components within a visualization [BG07b]. We addressed new ways to enrich the exploration of a visualization in adding aural feedback to the software visualization [BG08, BG09b]. On top of that, we implemented interaction capabilities with multitouch interfaces and basic speech recognition [BG10]. For a better integration within existing workflows, we addressed ways to automate and simplify the access to a software visualization [BG09a].

12.1 Acceptance of Hypotheses

Our research goals were investigated with a set of hypotheses. We briefly discuss their outcomes:

- *Cognitive metaphors permit an effective categorization of software entity* H1a: accepted

  We conducted a study with participants unfamiliar with the approach and looked if they were able to perceive characteristics of the software entity from the showed cognitive metaphor. The results showed that significantly more participants were able to distinguish between characteristics and based on that categorize the underlining software entities.

- *Cognitive metaphors allow a comparison of software entity* H1b: accepted

  We pair tested the results from the study to see if the participants were also able to distinguish characteristics between different cognitive metaphors. The tests showed that significantly more participants were able to compare different cognitive metaphors based on characteristics from the underlining software entities.

- *Sound can be used for accurate categorization of software entity* H2a: accepted

  In our study we asked participants to listen to sound samples and looked if they were able to perceive characteristics of the software entity out of the sample. The results showed that sound can be used to categorize software entities. Furthermore, samples with a cognitive metaphor (*e. g.* blubbering water) showed significantly better results than artificial sound samples.

- *Sound permits an accurate perception of the evolutionary changes of a software entity* H2b: accepted

  We asked participants to listen to a sequence of four tunes and looked if they were able to perceive evolutionary changes of the software entity. The results showed that for a set of characteristics significantly more participants were able to perceive the evolutionary changes as intended.

- *Surround sound guides an observer to a specific position in the visualization* H2c: accepted

  We asked participants to listen to a set of sound sample positioned in the space of a software visualization. Participants than were asked in which direction they would go if they were searching for a particular entity (*e. g.* a class with several bug reports). The results showed that significantly more participants where moving towards the intended direction.

- *Surround sound together with a force-directed layout allows perception of the stability of interconnected software entities.* H2d: accepted

  Other scientific work showed that force directed graphs can be used in software visualization to layout software entities based on their interconnectivity [FPG03]. We combined those results with the results from our studies regarding surround sound. In using stability metrics such as number of bug reports to create the aural feedback, we were able to guide users around a software visualization perceiving the stability of the interconnected software entities.

- *Multitouch gestures enable an adequate exploration of a software visualization* H3a: accepted

  During our user study we showed our participants different software situations and multitouch gestures. We than asked them to select the actions they would expect from this gesture. The results showed that all our actions needed for an adequate software exploration were associated with a gesture by the partecipants.

- *Adequate multitouch gesture mapping to interaction commands allows intuitive exploration* H3b: accepted

  We were able to show that for most gestures significantly more participants were expecting one particular command. An adequate mapping of gestures towards expected commands therefore results in less training and in a more intuitive exploration.

- *The use of spoken commands on a multitouch devices, allows to lower the need to access a keyboard* H4a: accepted

  With the use of spoken commands we are able to directly access macros, and automated comprehension tasks. This results in more automated steps and decreases the use of keyboard access.

12.2 Opportunities for Future Work

Based on the results of this dissertation, we see further promising research directions:

- *Cognitive glyphs*: As part of this dissertation we mainly focused on the house metaphor. Our short outlook towards other cognitive metaphors such as tables and spears showed that opportunities to improve visual perception could arise from them.

- *Metric Sets*: With our metric mixer we offer a way to combine analysis results from different fields. In creating adequate groups of such analysis results (Metric Sets) offers big potential to the benefits of cognitive glyphs.

- *Entity Audio*: We found evidence that the use of audio as an acceptable solution to access further information, without losing focus from the main software visualization. However, only basic use cases where analyzed as part of this work. The future steps are to concentrate on how detailed the audio feedback needs to be and which specific use cases benefit best from it.

- *Ambient Audio*: In this dissertation we showed only a proof-of-concept for the use of surround sound to guide an observer towards interesting parts in a software visualization. With our experiments we showed that these concepts offer big potentials for supported software exploration. For future work, these concepts could be adapted to specific use cases.

- *Automated Comprehension Tasks*: Within this work we showed our approach on automated configuration as an acceptable solution, to simplify the use of software exploration. The use of this configuration and macro mechanism for common use cases and tasks allow to lower the threshold of using software exploration to a minimum. Beyond that we showed that in adequately combining the automated tasks with our speechable commands we are able to leverage the approach even further.

- *Tactile Approach*: As part of this work we demonstrated the use of tactile devices as an intuitive and straightforward way to explore software systems. The proof-of-concept was limited to requirements for basic software exploration. Future work will focus on an adequate integration of interaction for advanced software exploration. We further plan to optimize the use of tactile devices for a collaborative environment with multiple observers and simultaneous interactions. Another direction is to address software exploration with the emerging stereoscopic technologies, were cameras are able to track interactions without any devices.

- *Collaborative Work*: With our support for software exploration on multitouch devices and first implementations on mobile devices, we are still at the beginning of a perfect integration of software exploration in a collaborative environment. We belief that such a combination leverages the benefits of collaboration in software engineering. Our future directions are therefore to address today's collaborative workflows in software engineering and optimize the use of our approach to these situations.

Part VI

Appendix

APPENDIX

Evaluation Questionnaire

In this Appendix we present the survey used during our evaluation. The survey is presented in its original language german.

Introduction Page 1

Liebe Teilnehmerin, lieber Teilnehmer

Bereits im Voraus vielen herzlichen Dank, dass Sie an der Studie zum Thema "Visualisierung" teilnehmen! Wir möchten mit dieser Studie Daten über die sinnvolle Verwendung von Visualisierungen sammeln.

Wichtig!!!: Bitte verwenden Sie **nicht den Opera-Browser** und stellen Sie jetzt sicher, dass Sie **die folgende Audio datei anhören** können

Hier sollte eine Quicktime datei erscheinen ---> `◀ ▶ ○━━━━━━━━ ◀ ▶ ▼` <---
ansonsten müssen Sie erst erst das Quicktime-Plugin installieren bevor Sie mit der Umfrage starten können

Die Studie dauert ca. 40 Minuten.

Introduction Page 2

⊙ Ich möchte ernsthaft an dieser Studie teilnehmen.

◯ Ich möchte mir nur einen Einblick in die Studie verschaffen.

Introduction Page 3

Allgemeine Hinweise:

- Wählen Sie zum Ausfüllen der Studie einen ruhigen Ort, wo Sie nicht gestört werden.
- Bitte lesen Sie die Instruktionen genau durch und lasse keine der Fragen aus.
- Bitte beantworten Sie alle Fragen ehrlich und wahrheitsgetreu. Seien Sie sich stets bewusst, dass es kein "richtig" oder "falsch" gibt und alle Angaben zu Ihrer Person anonym bleiben.

Introduction Page 4

Damit wir die verschiedenen Beiträge erkennen, Sie aber trotzdem anonym bleiben, sollten Sie nun noch Ihren **persönlichen Code** ausfüllen.

Zweiter Buchstabe deines Vornamens	Anfangsbuchstabe des Vornamens deiner Mutter	Anfangsbuchstabe deines Geburtsorts	Dein Geburtstag (ohne Monat & Jahr)
(Daniela)	(Monika)	(Uznach)	(28.07.1983)
A	M	U	28

Introduction Page 5

Fragen zu Ihrer Person

Geschlecht: ◯ w ◯ m

Alter:

Beruf:

Wie oft arbeitest Sie am Computer: ◯ täglich weniger als 4 Stunden
                                   ◯ täglich mehr als 4 Stunden
                                   ◯ alle zwei Tage ein mal
                                   ◯ weniger als zweimal pro Woche

Erfahrung	Keine	Beginner	Kenntnisreich	Fortgeschritten	Experte
Object-Orientiertes Programmieren	◯1	◯2	◯3	◯4	◯5
Java Programmieren	◯1	◯2	◯3	◯4	◯5
Gebrauch von Eclipse IDE	◯1	◯2	◯3	◯4	◯5
Reverse Engineering	◯1	◯2	◯3	◯4	◯5

Anzahl Jahre	Weniger als 1	1-3	4-6	6-10	Mehr als 10
Object-Orientiertes Programmieren	◯1	◯2	◯3	◯4	◯5
Java Programmieren	◯1	◯2	◯3	◯4	◯5
Gebrauch von Eclipse IDE	◯1	◯2	◯3	◯4	◯5
Reverse Engineering	◯1	◯2	◯3	◯4	◯5

SOFTWARE VISUALISIERUNG IM ALLTAG

Bevor Sie mit diesem Studienabschnitt beginnen können, möchten wir zunächst noch wissen, **wie Sie sich gerade jetzt in diesem Augenblick fühlen?** Sie können zwischen 9 Abstufungen wählen. Die Skala reicht von 1 = "sehr schlecht" bis 9 = "sehr gut".

☹ ◯1 ◯2 ◯3 ◯4 ◯5 ◯6 ◯7 ◯8 ◯9 ☺

sehr schlecht   sehr gut

MULTITOUCH ANSATZ
Multitouch Page MQ1

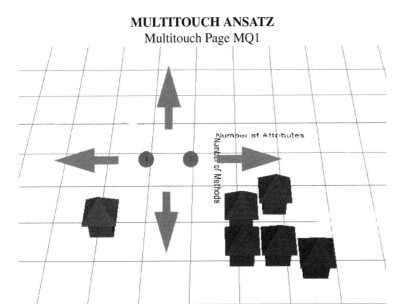

Mit zwei Finger gleichzeitig in die gleiche Richtung bewegen

Im Folgenden sehen Sie eine Liste von Aktionen. **Welche Aktionen würdesn Sie bei der Anwendung der gezeigten Geste auf die visualisierten Software Komponenten erwarten.** Beurteilen Sie in welchem Ausmass eher die linke oder eher die rechte Eigenschaft zutrifft. Je weiter die angekreuzte Zahl links von der Skalenmitte liegt, desto mehr trifft die linke Eigenschaft für Sie zu, und je weiter die angekreuzte Zahl rechts von der Skalenmitte liegt, desto mehr trifft die rechte Eigenschaft zu.

Vergrösserung (Zoom)	trifft nicht zu	○	○	○	○	○	○	○	○	trifft zu
Rotation	trifft nicht zu	○	○	○	○	○	○	○	○	trifft zu
Kontextmenu (Auswahlmenu)	trifft nicht zu	○	○	○	○	○	○	○	○	trifft zu
Layoutveränderung (Anordnung aller Komponenten verändern)	trifft nicht zu	○	○	○	○	○	○	○	○	trifft zu
Betrachtungs-positionsänderung (Kamera verschieben)	trifft nicht zu	○	○	○	○	○	○	○	○	trifft zu
Detailansicht (Information über eine Komponente)	trifft nicht zu	○	○	○	○	○	○	○	○	trifft zu
Historische Ansicht (Veränderungen über die zeit)	trifft nicht zu	○	○	○	○	○	○	○	○	trifft zu
Layout unabhängige Positionierung des Objektes (Verschieben einer Komponente)	trifft nicht zu	○	○	○	○	○	○	○	○	trifft zu

Multitouch Page MQ2

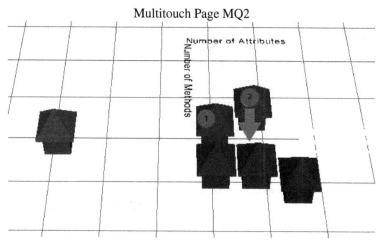

Mit einem Finger still berühren und den anderen bewegen

Im Folgenden sehen Sie eine Liste von Aktionen. **Welche Aktionen würdesn Sie bei der Anwendung der gezeigten Geste auf die visualisierten Software Komponenten erwarten.** Beurteilen Sie in welchem Ausmass eher die linke oder eher die rechte Eigenschaft zutrifft. Je weiter die angekreuzte Zahl links von der Skalenmitte liegt, desto mehr trifft die linke Eigenschaft für Sie zu, und je weiter die angekreuzte Zahl rechts von der Skalenmitte liegt, desto mehr trifft die rechte Eigenschaft zu.

Vergrösserung (Zoom)	trifft nicht zu	○	○	○	○	○	○	○	○	○	trifft zu
Rotation	trifft nicht zu	○	○	○	○	○	○	○	○	○	trifft zu
Kontextmenu (Auswahlmenu)	trifft nicht zu	○	○	○	○	○	○	○	○	○	trifft zu
Layoutveränderung (Anordnung aller Komponenten verändern)	trifft nicht zu	○	○	○	○	○	○	○	○	○	trifft zu
Betrachtungs- positionsänderung (Kamera verschieben)	trifft nicht zu	○	○	○	○	○	○	○	○	○	trifft zu
Detailansicht (Information über eine Komponente)	trifft nicht zu	○	○	○	○	○	○	○	○	○	trifft zu
Historische Ansicht (Veränderungen über die zeit)	trifft nicht zu	○	○	○	○	○	○	○	○	○	trifft zu
Layout unabhängige Positionierung des Objektes (Verschieben einer Komponente)	trifft nicht zu	○	○	○	○	○	○	○	○	○	trifft zu

Multitouch Page MQ3

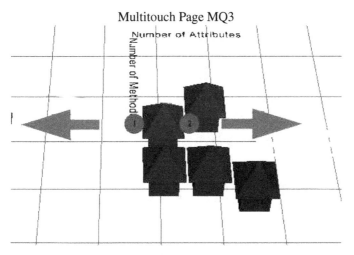

Mit zwei Fingern gleichzeitig in entgegengesetzter Richtung

Im Folgenden sehen Sie eine Liste von Aktionen. **Welche Aktionen würdesn Sie bei der Anwendung der gezeigten Geste auf die visualisierten Software Komponenten erwarten.** Beurteilen Sie in welchem Ausmass eher die linke oder eher die rechte Eigenschaft zutrifft. Je weiter die angekreuzte Zahl links von der Skalenmitte liegt, desto mehr trifft die linke Eigenschaft für Sie zu, und je weiter die angekreuzte Zahl rechts von der Skalenmitte liegt, desto mehr trifft die rechte Eigenschaft zu.

Vergrösserung (Zoom)	trifft nicht zu	O	O	O	O	O	O	O	O	trifft zu
Rotation	trifft nicht zu	O	O	O	O	O	O	O	O	trifft zu
Kontextmenu (Auswahlmenu)	trifft nicht zu	O	O	O	O	O	O	O	O	trifft zu
Layoutveränderung (Anordnung aller Komponenten verändern)	trifft nicht zu	O	O	O	O	O	O	O	O	trifft zu
Betrachtungs-positionsänderung (Kamera verschieben)	trifft nicht zu	O	O	O	O	O	O	O	O	trifft zu
Detailansicht (Information über eine Komponente)	trifft nicht zu	O	O	O	O	O	O	O	O	trifft zu
Historische Ansicht (Veränderungen über die zeit)	trifft nicht zu	O	O	O	O	O	O	O	O	trifft zu
Layout unabhängige Positionierung des Objektes (Verschieben einer Komponente)	trifft nicht zu	O	O	O	O	O	O	O	O	trifft zu

Multitouch Page MQ4

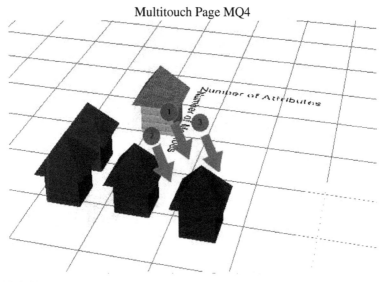

Mit drei Fingern bewegen

Im Folgenden sehen Sie eine Liste von Aktionen. **Welche Aktionen würdesn Sie bei der Anwendung der gezeigten Geste auf die visualisierten Software Komponenten erwarten.** Beurteilen Sie in welchem Ausmass eher die linke oder eher die rechte Eigenschaft zutrifft. Je weiter die angekreuzte Zahl links von der Skalenmitte liegt, desto mehr trifft die linke Eigenschaft für Sie zu, und je weiter die angekreuzte Zahl rechts von der Skalenmitte liegt, desto mehr trifft die rechte Eigenschaft zu.

Vergrösserung (Zoom)	trifft nicht zu	○ ○ ○ ○ ○ ○ ○ ○ ○							trifft zu
Rotation	trifft nicht zu	○ ○ ○ ○ ○ ○ ○ ○ ○							trifft zu
Kontextmenu (Auswahlmenu)	trifft nicht zu	○ ○ ○ ○ ○ ○ ○ ○ ○							trifft zu
Layoutveränderung (Anordnung aller Komponenten verändern)	trifft nicht zu	○ ○ ○ ○ ○ ○ ○ ○ ○							trifft zu
Betrachtungs-positionsänderung (Kamera verschieben)	trifft nicht zu	○ ○ ○ ○ ○ ○ ○ ○ ○							trifft zu
Detailansicht (Information über eine Komponente)	trifft nicht zu	○ ○ ○ ○ ○ ○ ○ ○ ○							trifft zu
Historische Ansicht (Veränderungen über die zeit)	trifft nicht zu	○ ○ ○ ○ ○ ○ ○ ○ ○							trifft zu
Layout unabhängige Positionierung des Objektes (Verschieben einer Komponente)	trifft nicht zu	○ ○ ○ ○ ○ ○ ○ ○ ○							trifft zu

Multitouch Page MQ5

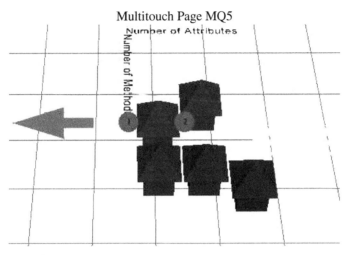

Swipe (streifen, wischen, bewegen) mit zwei Fingern nach links

Im Folgenden sehen Sie eine Liste von Aktionen. **Welche Aktionen würdesn Sie bei der Anwendung der gezeigten Geste auf die visualisierten Software Komponenten erwarten.** Beurteilen Sie in welchem Ausmass eher die linke oder eher die rechte Eigenschaft zutrifft. Je weiter die angekreuzte Zahl links von der Skalenmitte liegt, desto mehr trifft die linke Eigenschaft für Sie zu, und je weiter die angekreuzte Zahl rechts von der Skalenmitte liegt, desto mehr trifft die rechte Eigenschaft zu.

Vergrösserung (Zoom)	trifft nicht zu	○	○	○	○	○	○	○	○	trifft zu
Rotation	trifft nicht zu	○	○	○	○	○	○	○	○	trifft zu
Kontextmenu (Auswahlmenu)	trifft nicht zu	○	○	○	○	○	○	○	○	trifft zu
Layoutveränderung (Anordnung aller Komponenten verändern)	trifft nicht zu	○	○	○	○	○	○	○	○	trifft zu
Betrachtungs- positionsänderung (Kamera verschieben)	trifft nicht zu	○	○	○	○	○	○	○	○	trifft zu
Detailansicht (Information über eine Komponente)	trifft nicht zu	○	○	○	○	○	○	○	○	trifft zu
Historische Ansicht (Veränderungen über die zeit)	trifft nicht zu	○	○	○	○	○	○	○	○	trifft zu
Layout unabhängige Positionierung des Objektes (Verschieben einer Komponente)	trifft nicht zu	○	○	○	○	○	○	○	○	trifft zu

Multitouch Page MQ6

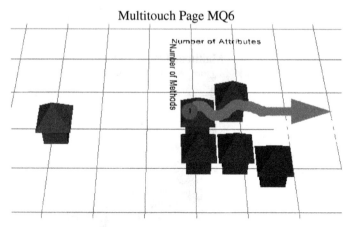

Wellenbewegung mit einem Finger nach rechts

Im Folgenden sehen Sie eine Liste von Aktionen. **Welche Aktionen würdesn Sie bei der Anwendung der gezeigten Geste auf die visualisierten Software Komponenten erwarten.** Beurteilen Sie in welchem Ausmass eher die linke oder eher die rechte Eigenschaft zutrifft. Je weiter die angekreuzte Zahl links von der Skalenmitte liegt, desto mehr trifft die linke Eigenschaft für Sie zu, und je weiter die angekreuzte Zahl rechts von der Skalenmitte liegt, desto mehr trifft die rechte Eigenschaft zu.

Vergrösserung (Zoom)	trifft nicht zu	○	○	○	○	○	○	○	○	trifft zu
Rotation	trifft nicht zu	○	○	○	○	○	○	○	○	trifft zu
Kontextmenu (Auswahlmenu)	trifft nicht zu	○	○	○	○	○	○	○	○	trifft zu
Layoutveränderung (Anordnung aller Komponenten verändern)	trifft nicht zu	○	○	○	○	○	○	○	○	trifft zu
Betrachtungs-positionsänderung (Kamera verschieben)	trifft nicht zu	○	○	○	○	○	○	○	○	trifft zu
Detailansicht (Information über eine Komponente)	trifft nicht zu	○	○	○	○	○	○	○	○	trifft zu
Historische Ansicht (Veränderungen über die zeit)	trifft nicht zu	○	○	○	○	○	○	○	○	trifft zu
Layout unabhängige Positionierung des Objektes (Verschieben einer Komponente)	trifft nicht zu	○	○	○	○	○	○	○	○	trifft zu

Bevor Sie mit diesem Studienabschnitt beginnen können, möchten wir zunächst noch wissen, **wie Sie sich gerade jetzt in diesem Augenblick fühlen?** Sie können zwischen 9 Abstufungen wählen. Die Skala reicht von 1 = "sehr schlecht" bis 9 = "sehr gut".

sehr schlecht   sehr gut

AUDIO UNTERSTÜTZTER ANSATZ

Hör Sie sich die Audiodatei an und klicken Sie dann weiter.

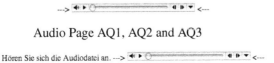

Audio Page AQ1, AQ2 and AQ3

Hören Sie sich die Audiodatei an. --->

Im Folgenden sehen Sie eine Liste von Eigenschaften. **Welche Eigenschaften würden Sie der gehörten Software Komponente geben.** Beurteilen Sie in welchem Ausmass eher die linke oder eher die rechte Eigenschaft zutrifft. Je weiter die angekreuzte Zahl links von der Skalenmitte liegt, desto mehr trifft die linke Eigenschaft für Sie zu, und je weiter die angekreuzte Zahl rechts von der Skalenmitte liegt, desto mehr trifft die rechte Eigenschaft zu.

Wie finden Sie das Gehörte(Wenn Sie nicht weiter wissen dann nehmen Sie keine Angabe)

einfach	O	O	O	O	O	O	O	O	complex	keine Angabe
klein	O	O	O	O	O	O	O	O	umfangreich	keine Angabe
erweckt Interesse	O	O	O	O	O	O	O	O	uninteressant	keine Angabe
ruhig	O	O	O	O	O	O	O	O	lebhaft	keine Angabe
experimentierfreudig	O	O	O	O	O	O	O	O	an Bewährtem orientiert	keine Angabe
phantasievoll	O	O	O	O	O	O	O	O	nüchtern	keine Angabe
fehler behaftet	O	O	O	O	O	O	O	O	fehlerfrei	keine Angabe
unabhängig	O	O	O	O	O	O	O	O	abhängig	keine Angabe
widerstandsfähig	O	O	O	O	O	O	O	O	schwach	keine Angabe

Für Informatiker (Wenn Sie nicht weiter wissen dann nehmen Sie keine Angabe)											
schlecht designed	○	○	○	○	○	○	○	○	○	gut designed	○ keine Angabe
geringe Anzahl Codezeilen	○	○	○	○	○	○	○	○	○	viele Codezeilen	○ keine Angabe
geringe Anzahl Methoden	○	○	○	○	○	○	○	○	○	viele Methoden	○ keine Angabe
ist keine Klasse	○	○	○	○	○	○	○	○	○	ist eine Klasse	○ keine Angabe
ist keine Methode	○	○	○	○	○	○	○	○	○	ist eine Methode	○ keine Angabe
wenig Änderungen	○	○	○	○	○	○	○	○	○	viele Änderungen	○ keine Angabe
alte Komponente	○	○	○	○	○	○	○	○	○	neue Komponente	○ keine Angabe

Intermediate Audio Page

Bevor Sie mit diesem Studienabschnitt beginnen können, möchten wir zunächst noch wissen, **wie Sie sich gerade jetzt in diesem Augenblick fühlen?** Sie können zwischen 9 Abstufungen wählen. Die Skala reicht von 1 = "sehr schlecht" bis 9 = "sehr gut".

😟 ○1 ○2 ○3 ○4 ○5 ○6 ○7 ○8 ○9 😃

sehr schlecht   sehr gut

Audio Page AQ4 - AQ9

Hören Sie sich die Audiodatei an. --->  <---

Im Folgenden sehen Sie eine Liste von Eigenschaften. **Welche Eigenschaften würden Sie der gehörten Software Komponente geben.** Beurteilen Sie in welchem Ausmass eher die linke oder eher die rechte Eigenschaft zutrifft. Je weiter die angekreuzte Zahl links von der Skalenmitte liegt, desto mehr trifft die linke Eigenschaft für Sie zu, und je weiter die angekreuzte Zahl rechts von der Skalenmitte liegt, desto mehr trifft die rechte Eigenschaft zu.

Wie finden Sie das Gehörte(Wenn Sie nicht weiter wissen dann nehmen Sie keine Angabe)

einfach	○	○	○	○	○	○	○	○	○	complex	keine Angabe
klein	○	○	○	○	○	○	○	○	○	umfangreich	keine Angabe
erweckt Interesse	○	○	○	○	○	○	○	○	○	uninteressant	keine Angabe
ruhig	○	○	○	○	○	○	○	○	○	lebhaft	keine Angabe
experimentierfreudig	○	○	○	○	○	○	○	○	○	an Bewährtem orientiert	keine Angabe
phantasievoll	○	○	○	○	○	○	○	○	○	nüchtern	keine Angabe
fehler behaftet	○	○	○	○	○	○	○	○	○	fehlerfrei	keine Angabe
unabhängig	○	○	○	○	○	○	○	○	○	abhängig	keine Angabe
widerstandsfähig	○	○	○	○	○	○	○	○	○	schwach	keine Angabe

Für Informatiker (Wenn Sie nicht weiter wissen dann nehmen Sie keine Angabe)

schlecht designed	○	○	○	○	○	○	○	○	○	gut designed	keine Angabe
geringe Anzahl Codezeilen	○	○	○	○	○	○	○	○	○	viele Codezeilen	keine Angabe
geringe Anzahl Methoden	○	○	○	○	○	○	○	○	○	viele Methoden	keine Angabe
ist keine Klasse	○	○	○	○	○	○	○	○	○	ist eine Klasse	keine Angabe
ist keine Methode	○	○	○	○	○	○	○	○	○	ist eine Methode	keine Angabe
wenig Änderungen	○	○	○	○	○	○	○	○	○	viele Änderungen	keine Angabe
alte Komponente	○	○	○	○	○	○	○	○	○	neue Komponente	keine Angabe

Intermediate Audio Page

Bevor Sie mit diesem Studienabschnitt beginnen können, möchten wir zunächst noch wissen, **wie Sie sich gerade jetzt in diesem Augenblick fühlen?** Sie können zwischen 9 Abstufungen wählen. Die Skala reicht von 1 = "sehr schlecht" bis 9 = "sehr gut".

sehr schlecht   sehr gut

Audio Page AQ10

Sie sind auf der Suche nach **vielen Fehlern**. Wenn Sie die folgenden Geräusche hören, zu welchem Punkt würden Sie sich vom blauen Marker aus bewegen

Bei Punkt 1 hören Sie

Bei Punkt 2 hören Sie

Bei Punkt 3 hören Sie

- ○ Sie schieben den Marker in Richtung 1
- ○ Sie schieben den Marker in Richtung 2
- ○ Sie schieben den Marker in Richtung 3
- ○ Sie schieben den Marker in Richtung 4

Audio Page AQ11

Sie sind auf der Suche nach **Häusern, welche wenige Veränderungen erhalten haben**. Wenn Sie die folgenden Geräusche hören, zu welchem Punkt würden Sie sich vom blauen Marker aus bewegen

Bei Punkt 2 hören Sie

Bei Punkt 3 hören Sie

Bei Punkt 4 hören Sie

- Sie schieben den Marker in Richtung 1
- Sie schieben den Marker in Richtung 2
- Sie schieben den Marker in Richtung 3
- Sie schieben den Marker in Richtung 4

VISUELLER ANSATZ

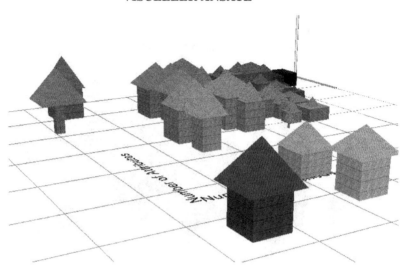

Ihnen wurde der Ansatz von CocoViz zugelost. Schauen Sie sich das Bild an, damit Sie mit den unterschiedlichen Objekten der Visualisierung mit diesem Ansatz vertraut sind. Solche Objekte stellen virtuelle Daten dar (z.B Software). Es müssen nicht alle folgenden Antworten für diesen Ansatz Sinn machen, versuchen Sie trotzdem gewissenhaft zu antworten

Visual Objects used for VQ1, VQ2 and VQ3

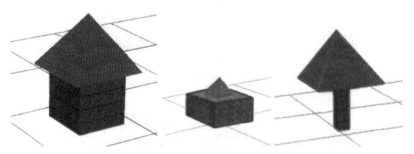

Im Folgenden sehen Sie eine Liste von Eigenschaften. **Welche Eigenschaften würden Sie der gezeigten visualisierten Software Komponente geben.**
Beurteilen Sie in welchem Ausmass eher die linke oder eher die rechte Eigenschaft zutrifft. Je weiter die angekreuzte Zahl links von der Skalenmitte liegt, desto mehr trifft die linke Eigenschaft für Sie zu, und je weiter die angekreuzte Zahl rechts von der Skalenmitte liegt, desto mehr trifft die rechte Eigenschaft zu.

Wie empfinden Sie das gezeigte Object(Wenn Sie nicht weiter wissen dann nehmen Sie keine Angabe)

einfach	○	○	○	○	○	○	○	○	○	complex	keine Angabe
klein	○	○	○	○	○	○	○	○	○	umfangreich	keine Angabe
erweckt Interesse	○	○	○	○	○	○	○	○	○	uninteressant	keine Angabe
phantasievoll	○	○	○	○	○	○	○	○	○	nüchtern	keine Angabe
experimentierfreudig	○	○	○	○	○	○	○	○	○	an Bewährtem orientiert	keine Angabe
unabhängig	○	○	○	○	○	○	○	○	○	abhängig	keine Angabe
widerstandsfähig	○	○	○	○	○	○	○	○	○	schwach	keine Angabe

Für Informatiker (Wenn Sie nicht weiter wissen dann nehmen Sie keine Angabe)

geringe Anzahl Codezeilen	○	○	○	○	○	○	○	○	○	viele Codezeilen	keine Angabe
geringe Anzahl Methoden	○	○	○	○	○	○	○	○	○	viele Methoden	keine Angabe
ist keine Klasse	○	○	○	○	○	○	○	○	○	ist eine Klasse	keine Angabe
ist keine Methode	○	○	○	○	○	○	○	○	○	ist eine Methode	keine Angabe
fehler behaftet	○	○	○	○	○	○	○	○	○	fehlerfrei	keine Angabe
alte Komponente	○	○	○	○	○	○	○	○	○	neue Komponente	keine Angabe
wenig Änderungen	○	○	○	○	○	○	○	○	○	viele Änderungen	keine Angabe
schlecht designed	○	○	○	○	○	○	○	○	○	gut designed	keine Angabe

VISUELLER ANSATZ (Vergleich)

Wir vergleichen nun zwei unterschiedliche Ansätze. Schauen Sie sich die Bilder an, damit Sie mit den unterschiedlichen Objekten einer Visualisierung der Ansäte vertraut sind. Solche Objekte stellen wieder virtuelle Daten dar (z.B Software). Es müssen nicht alle folgenden Antworten für diese Ansätze Sinn machen, versuchen Sie trotzdem gewissenhaft zu antworten

Visual Page VQ4

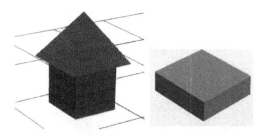

Sie sehen zwei verschiedene Software Visualisierungsansätze. Vergleichen Sie den **ersten** mit dem zweiten.

Welche Eigenschaften würden Sie der ersten visualisierten Software Komponente eher geben.

Beurteilen Sie in welchem Ausmass eher die linke oder eher die rechte Eigenschaft zutrifft. Je weiter die angekreuzte Zahl links von der Skalenmitte liegt, desto mehr trifft die linke Eigenschaft für Sie zu, und je weiter die angekreuzte Zahl rechts von der Skalenmitte liegt, desto mehr trifft die rechte Eigenschaft zu.

Wie empfinden Sie das gezeigte Object(Wenn Sie nicht weiter wissen dann nehmen Sie keine Angabe)

einfacher	○	○	○	○	○	○	○	○	○	complexer	○ keine Angabe
kleiner	○	○	○	○	○	○	○	○	○	umfangreich	○ keine Angabe
erweckt mehr Interesse	○	○	○	○	○	○	○	○	○	uninteressanter	○ keine Angabe
phantasievoller	○	○	○	○	○	○	○	○	○	nüchterner	○ keine Angabe
experimentierfreudiger	○	○	○	○	○	○	○	○	○	an Bewährtem orientierter	○ keine Angabe
unabhängiger	○	○	○	○	○	○	○	○	○	abhängiger	○ keine Angabe
widerstandsfähiger	○	○	○	○	○	○	○	○	○	schwächer	○ keine Angabe

Für Informatiker (Wenn Sie nicht weiter wissen dann nehmen Sie keine Angabe)

geringere Anzahl Codezeilen	○	○	○	○	○	○	○	○	○	mehr Codezeilen	○ keine Angabe
geringere Anzahl Methoden	○	○	○	○	○	○	○	○	○	mehr Methoden	○ keine Angabe
ist eher keine Klasse	○	○	○	○	○	○	○	○	○	ist eher eine Klasse	○ keine Angabe
ist eher keine Methode	○	○	○	○	○	○	○	○	○	ist eher eine Methode	○ keine Angabe
fehler behafteter	○	○	○	○	○	○	○	○	○	fehlerfreier	○ keine Angabe
ältere Komponente	○	○	○	○	○	○	○	○	○	neuere Komponente	○ keine Angabe
weniger Änderungen	○	○	○	○	○	○	○	○	○	mehr Änderungen	○ keine Angabe
schlechter designed	○	○	○	○	○	○	○	○	○	besser designed	○ keine Angabe

Intermediate Visual Page

Bevor Sie mit diesem Studienabschnitt beginnen können, möchten wir zunächst noch wissen, **wie Sie sich gerade jetzt in diesem Augenblick fühlen?** Sie können zwischen 9 Abstufungen wählen. Die Skala reicht von 1 = "sehr schlecht" bis 9 = "sehr gut".

☹ ○1 ○2 ○3 ○4 ○5 ○6 ○7 ○8 ○9 ☺

sehr schlecht   sehr gut

Final Page 1

Wie motiviert waren Sie, die Aufgabe zu bearbeiten?

überhaupt nicht motiviert ○1 ○2 ○3 ○4 ○5 ○6 ○7 ○8 ○9 sehr motiviert

Wie wichtig war es für Sie, in dieser Aufgabe gut abzuschneiden?

überhaupt nicht wichtig ○1 ○2 ○3 ○4 ○5 ○6 ○7 ○8 ○9 sehr wichtig

Wie schwierig war die Aufgabe?

überhaupt nicht schwierig ○1 ○2 ○3 ○4 ○5 ○6 ○7 ○8 ○9 sehr schwierig

Wie gut glauben Sie, haben Sie in dieser Aufgabe abgeschnitten?

sehr schlecht ○1 ○2 ○3 ○4 ○5 ○6 ○7 ○8 ○9 sehr gut

Final Page 2

Ich habe mich beim Bearbeiten der Fragebögen genau an die Anweisungen gehalten und die Fragen ehrlich beantwortet?

○Ja ○Nein

Ich wurde beim Bearbeiten der Fragen gestört oder unterbrochen?

○Ja ○Nein

Hast Du noch allgemeine Anmerkungen oder Kommentare zu einem der bearbeiteten Fragebögen?

Final Page 3

Vielen herzlichen Dank!

Falls Sie Fragen haben, können Sie sich gerne an Sandro Boccuzzo boccuzzo (at) ifi.uzh.ch wenden.

B

Glossary

Ambient Audio: An audio feedback using surround sound technologies. The feedback represents the atmosphere of a situation at a particular position in an software visualization. It is generated out of several overlaying entity audio feedback's played from the position where the representing software entity is visualized.

Ambient Audio Software Exploration (AASE): AASE extends the audio support for software visualizations, with assisted navigation, a space annotated with sounds (AEP) and perception of entities with dependencies to a more explorative modality.

Audio Exploration Path (AEP): When using ambient audio, the audio feedback is constantly adapting to the situation of the new position. An observer acting to these changes is leat on a trail. We refer to this trail as an audio exploration path.

Automated Comprehension task: A automated comprehension task is a set of configurations and macros that allow a simple creation of a adequate software visualization with regard to a common software comprehension task.

Cognitive glyphs: Cognitive glyphs are visual objects known from our daily live such as a house, where metrics can be mapped to change its look. (*e.g.* metrics affect the roof and the body of the house metaphor).

Entity Audio: An audio feedback that represents a secondary characteristic of the visualized software entity.

Famix: Famix is a language independent meta-model developed in the EU project FAMOOS [DTP99].

Metric Cluster: Metric Cluster is a set of metrics that together allow one to adequately answer a particular software visualization question.

MVC: Stands for Model-View-Controller a design approach described in [Ree79].

Pinch Gesture: A pinch gesture in general referees to a gesture where two fingers are pinched together. The most common use is to zoom-in or zoom-out in a graphical context.

Software Exploration: Navigation, interaction and analysis of a presented software visualization.

Software Visualization: Presenting the abstract characteristics of a software project in an understandable form.

SV-Mixer: Software-Visualization Mixer. Similar to a audio-mixer in the music industry. It allows to filter and configure the mappings of metrics and their visual representation.

Swipe Gesture: A swipe gesture in general referees to a gesture where two fingers are moved together to the left or to the right.

Publications

This appendix present the list of publications on which this dissertation is based on.

C.1 Conference Papers

On entity audio: [BG08] Sandro Boccuzzo, Harald C. Gall, Software Visualization with Audio Supported Cognitive Glyphs, 24th IEEE International Conference on Software Maintenance (ICSM 2008) 2008, IEEE Computer Society. (inproceedings)

On ambient audio: [BG09b] Sandro Boccuzzo, Harald C. Gall, CocoViz with ambient audio software exploration, ICSE '09: Proceedings of the 2009 IEEE 31st International Conference on Software Engineering 2009. (inproceedings)

On automated tasks: [BG09a] Sandro Boccuzzo, Harald C. Gall, Automated Comprehension Tasks in Software Exploration, ASE '09: Proceedings of the 2009 International Conference on Automated Software Engineering 2009. (inproceedings/Short Paper)

On multitouch: [BG10] Sandro Boccuzzo, Harald C. Gall, Multi-Touch Collaboration for Software Exploration, Proceedings of the International Conference on Program Comprehension (ICPC'10) 2010. (inproceedings)

C.2 Workshop Papers

On cognitive glyphs: [BG07b] Sandro Boccuzzo, Harald C. Gall, CocoViz: Towards Cognitive Software Visualizations, Proceedings of IEEE International Workshop on Visualizing Software for Understanding and Analysis (VisSoft 2007) 2007, IEEE Computer Society. (inproceedings)

On cognitive glyphs: [BG07a] Sandro Boccuzzo, Harald C. Gall, CocoViz: Supported Cognitive Software Visualization, Proceedings of 14th Working Conference on Reverse Engineering (WCRE 2007) 2007, IEEE Computer Society. (inproceedings)

C.3 Technical Reports

On the results of the first project: [BW⁺09] Sandro Boccuzzo, Richard Wettel, Sazzadul Alam, Philippe Dugerdil, Harald C. Gall, Michele Lanza, EvoSpaces - Multi-dimentional Navigation Spaces for Software Evolution Vol. LNCS 5440, Springer 2009. (inbook)

Bibliography

[AM08]   Brian de Alwis and Gail C. Murphy. Answering conceptual queries
           with ferret. In *Proc. Int'l Conf. on Softw. Eng. (ICSE)*, pages 21–30,
           2008.

[Bar03]   Stephan Barrass. Sonification design patterns. In *Proc. Int'l Conf. on
           Auditory Display*, 2003.

[BD04]   M. Balzer and O. Deussen. Hierarchy based 3d visualization of large
           software structures. In *Int'l Conf. on Visualization*, 2004.

[BDA97]   Ron Baecker, Chris DiGiano, and Marcus Aaron. Software visual-
           ization for debugging. *Commun. ACM*, 40(4):44–54, 1997.

[BDGG06]   Lewis Berman, Sebastian Danicic, Keith Gallagher, and Nicolas
           Gold. The sound of software: Using sonification to aid comprehen-
           sion. In *Proc. IEEE Int'l Conf. on Program Comprehension*, pages
           225–229, 2006.

[BDL05]   Michael Balzer, Oliver Deussen, and Claus Lewerentz. Voronoi
           treemaps for the visualization of software metrics. In *Proc. ACM
           Symp. on Softw. visualization*, pages 165–172, 2005.

[BE96]   T. Ball and S. G. Eick. Software visualization in the large. *Computer*,
           29(4):33–43, 1996.

[BG06]   Lewis I. Berman and Keith B. Gallagher. Listening to program slices.
           In *Proc. Int'l Conf. on Auditory Display*, 2006.

[BG07a]   Sandro Boccuzzo and Harald C. Gall. Cocoviz: Supported cogni-
           tive software visualization. In *Proc. Working Conf. on Reverse Eng.*,
           2007.

[BG07b]   Sandro Boccuzzo and Harald C. Gall. Cocoviz: Towards cognitive
           software visualization. In *Proc. IEEE Int'l Workshop on Visualizing
           Softw. for Understanding and Analysis*, 2007.

[BG08]   Sandro Boccuzzo and Harald C. Gall. Software visualization with au-
           dio supported cognitive glyphs. In *Proc. Int'l Conf. on Softw. Main-
           tenance*, 2008.

[BG09a]   Sandro Boccuzzo and Harald C. Gall. Automated comprehension tasks in software exploration. In *Proc. Int'l Conf. on Automated Softw. Eng. (ASE)*, 2009.

[BG09b]   Sandro Boccuzzo and Harald C. Gall. Cocoviz with ambient audio software exploration. In *Proc. Int'l Conf. on Softw. Eng. (ICSE)*, 2009.

[BG10]   Sandro Boccuzzo and Harald C. Gall. Multi-touch collaboration for software exploration. In *Proc. Int'l Conf. on Program Comprehension (ICPC)*, 2010.

[BH91]   M.H. Brown and J. Hershberger. Colour and sound in algorithm animation. In *Proc. IEEE Workshop on Visual Languages*, pages 52–63, 1991.

[BKH05]   F. Bendix, R. Kosara, and H. Hauser. Parallel sets: visual analysis of categorical data. *IEEE Symp. on Info. Visualization*, pages 133–140, 2005.

[BW⁺09]   Sandro Boccuzzo, , Richard Wettel, Sazzadul Alam, Philippe Dugerdil, Harald C. Gall, and Michele Lanza. *EvoSpaces - Multidimensional Navigation Spaces for Software Evolution*, chapter 3, pages 167–192. Springer, 2009.

[CCKT83]   John Chambers, William Cleveland, Beat Kleiner, and Paul Tukey. Graphical methods for data analysis, wadsworth. 1983.

[Che73]   Herman Chernoff. The use of faces to represent points in k-dimensional space graphically. volume 68, pages 361–368, 1973.

[CSD⁺92]   Carolina Cruz-Neira, Daniel J. Sandin, Thomas A. DeFanti, Robert V. Kenyon, and John C. Hart. The cave: audio visual experience automatic virtual environment. *Commun. ACM*, 35(6):64–72, 1992.

[DA07]   Philippe Dugerdil and Sazzadul Alam. Evospaces: 3d visualization of software architecture. In *Proc. IEEE Int'l Conf. on Softw. Eng. and Knowledge Eng.*, 2007.

[DA08]   Philippe Dugerdil and Sazzadul Alam. Execution trace visualization in a 3d space. In *Proc. Int'l Conf. on Information Technology*, 2008.

[DBO93] Christopher J. DiGiano, Ronald M. Baecker, and Russell N. Owen. Logomedia: a sound-enhanced programming environment for monitoring program behavior. In *Proc. Conf. on Human factors in computing systems*, pages 301–302, 1993.

[DE01] Raimund Dachselt and Jurgen Ebert. Collapsible cylindrical trees: A fast hierarchical navigation technique. *IEEE Symp. on Info. Visualization*, pages 79–86, 2001.

[DFG99] Q. Du, V. Faber, and M. Gunzburger. Centroidal voronoi tessellations: Applications and algorithms. *SIAM Review*, 41:637–676, 1999.

[DL01] Paul Dietz and Darren Leigh. Diamondtouch: A multi-user touch technology. In *UIST*, pages 219–226, November 2001.

[DTP99] Serge Demeyer, S. Tichelaarand, and Steyaert P. Famix2.0-the famoos information exchange model. In *Technical Report, University of Berne*, 1999.

[ES98] K. Erdos and H. M. Sneed. Partial comprehension of complex programs. In *Proc. Int'l Workshop on Program Comprehension*, pages 98–105, 1998.

[ESS92] Stephen G. Eick, Joseph L. Steffen, and Eric E. Sumner, Jr. Seesoft - a tool for visualizing line oriented software statistics. *IEEE Trans. Softw. Eng.*, 18(11):957–968, 1992.

[FBB+99] Martin Fowler, Kent Beck, John Brant, William Opdyke, and Don Roberts. *Refactoring: Improving the Design of Existing Code*. Addison Wesley, 1999.

[FCI05] Elena Fanea, Sheelagh Carpendale, and Tobias Isenberg. An interactive 3d integration of parallel coordinates and star glyphs. *IEEE Symp. on Info. Visualization*, pages 149–156, 2005.

[Fie79] Stephen E. Fienberg. Graphical methods in statistics. 33(4):165–178, nov 1979.

[FM05] Louise J. Finlayson and Chris Mellish. The audioview - providing a glance at java source code. In *Proc. Int'l Conf. on Auditory Display*, 2005.

[FPG03]   Michael Fischer, Martin Pinzger, and Harald Gall. Populating a re-
           lease history database from version control and bug tracking systems.
           In *Proc. Int'l Conf. on Softw. Maintenance*, pages 23–32, 2003.

[FR81a]   Bernhard Flury and Hans Riedwyl. Graphical representation of mul-
           tivariante data by means of asymmetrical faces. volume 76, pages
           757–765, 1981.

[FR81b]   Bernhard Flury and Hans Riedwyl. Graphical representation of mul-
           tivariate data by means of asymmetrical faces. In *Journal of the
           American Statistical Association Journal of the American Statistical
           Association Vol. 76, No. 376*, pages 757–765, 1981.

[FWR99]   Ying-Huey Fua, Matthew O. Ward, and Elke A. Rundensteiner. Hi-
           erarchical parallel coordinates for exploration of large datasets. In
           Proc. Conf. on Visualization, pages 43–50, 1999.

[GFP09]   Harald C. Gall, Beat Fluri, and Martin Pinzger. Change Analysis
           with Evolizer and ChangeDistiller. *IEEE Software*, 26(1):26–33, Jan-
           uary/February 2009.

[GG03]   D. Gentner and S. Goldin-Meadow. Why we're so smart. In *Lan-
           guage in mind: Advances in the study of language and thought*, pages
           195–235, 2003.

[GHJ98]   H. Gall, K. Hajek, and M. Jazayeri. Detection of logical coupling
           based on product release history. In *Proc. Int'l Conf. on Softw. Main-
           tenance*, pages 190–198, Nov 1998.

[GJR99]   Harald Gall, Mehdi Jazayeri, and Claudio Riva. Visualizing software
           release histories: The use of color and third dimension. In *Proc. Int'l
           Conf. on Software Maintenance (ICSM)*, pages 99–108, 1999.

[Gos60]   K. L. Gosner. *A simplified table for staging anuran embryos and
           larvae with notes on identification*. Addison Wesley, 1960.

[Gru94]   Jonathan Grudin. CSCW: History and focus. In *IEEE Computer, 27,
           5*,, pages 19–26, 1994.

[Hal77]   Maurice H. Halstead. *Elements of software science, operating and
           programming system series*. Elsevier, 7, 1977.

[Han05]   Jefferson Y. Han. Low-cost multi-touch sensing through frustrated total internal reflection. In *Proc. of ACM symposium on User Interface Software and Technology*, 2005.

[HE99]   C. G. Healey and J. T. Enns. Large datasets at a glance: combining textures and colors in scientific visualization. *IEEE Trans. on Visualization and Computer Graphics*, 5(2):145–167, 1999.

[Hil98]   S. Hiltz. Collaborative learning in asynchronous learning networks: Building learning communities. In *Web 98 Symposium*, 1998.

[Hin87]   H. Hinterberger. *Data density: a powerful abstraction to manage and analyze multivariate data*. ETH Zurich, No.4, 1987, 1987.

[HP96]   Richard Holt and Jason Pak. Gase: Visualizing software evolution-in-the-large. In *Proc. Working Conf. on Reverse Engineering (WCRE)*, pages 163–167, 1996.

[HTB$^+$07] Otmar Hilliges, Lucia Terrenghi, Sebastian Boring, David Kim, Hendrik Richter, and Andreas Butz. Designing for collaborative creative problem solving. In *C&C '07: Proc. Conf. on creativity & cognition*, pages 137–146, 2007.

[ID90]   A. Inselberg and B. Dimsdale. Parallel coordinates: a tool for visualizing multi-dimensional geometry. In *Proc. IEEE Conf. on Visualization*, pages 361–378, 1990.

[JCJ05]   J. Johansson, M. Cooper, and M. Jern. 3-dimensional display for clustered multi-relational parallel coordinates. *Int'l Conf. on Info. Visualization*, pages 188–193, 2005.

[JDV03]   Doug Janzen and Kris De Volder. Navigating and querying code without getting lost. In *Proc. Int'l Conf. on Aspect-oriented Softw. development*, pages 178–187, 2003.

[JS91]   B. Johnson and B. Shneiderman. Tree-maps: a space-filling approach to the visualization of hierarchical information structures. In *Proc. IEEE Conf. on Visualization*, pages 284–291, 1991.

[KB07]   Martin Kaltenbrunner and Ross Bencina. reactivision: a computer-vision framework for table-based tangible interaction. In *TEI '07: Proc. Int'l Conf. on Tangible and Embedded Interaction*, pages 69–74, 2007.

[KBBC05]   M. Kaltenbrunner, T. Bovermann, R. Bencina, and E. Costanza. Tuio: A protocol for table-top tangible user interfaces. In *Proc. Int'l Workshop on Gesture in Human-Computer Interaction and Simulation*, 2005.

[KLN08]   Adrian Kuhn, Peter Loretan, and Oscar Nierstrasz. Consistent layout for thematic software maps. In *Proc. of Working Conference on Reverse Engineering (WCRE08)*, page 209–218, 2008.

[Kvv01]   E. Kleiberg, H. van de Wetering, and J.J. van Wijk. Botanical visualization of huge hierarchies. *IEEE Symp. on Info. Visualization*, pages 87–94, 2001.

[LA95]   Johnson W. L. and Erdem A. Interactive explanation of software systems. In *Proc. Knowledge-Based Softw. Eng. (KBSE)*, pages 155–164, 1995.

[Lak93]   A. Lakhotia. Understanding someone else's code: Analysis and experience. In *Journal of Systems and Software, 23(3)*, pages 269–275, 1993.

[Lan01]   Michele Lanza. The evolution matrix: recovering software evolution using software visualization techniques. In *Proc. Int'l Workshop on Principles of Softw. Evolution*, pages 37–42, 2001.

[LBS85]   SK. Lee, W. Buxon, and K. C. Smith. A multi-touch three dimensional touch-sensitive tablet. In *Proc. of the ACM Conf. on Human Factors in Computing Systems (CHI'85)*, pages 21–25, April 1985.

[LD02]   Michele Lanza and Stéphane Ducasse. Understanding software evolution using a combination of software visualization and software metrics. In *Proc. of Langages et Modèles á Objets (LMO 2002)*, pages 135–149, 2002.

[LD03]   Michele Lanza and Stéphane Ducasse. Polymetric views — a lightweight visual approach to reverse engineering. *IEEE Trans. on Softw. Eng.*, 29(9):782–795, 2003.

[Let98]   S. Letovsky. Cognitive processes in program comprehension. In *The Journal of Systems and Software, 7(4)*, pages 325–339, 1998.

[LJ80]   G. Lakoff and M. Johnson. *Metaphors we live by*. Chicago: University of Chicago Press., 1980.

[LK97]   Chang Hong Liu and John M. Kennedy. Form symbolism, analogy, and metaphor. In *Psychonomic Bulletin and Review 4 (4)*, pages 546–551, 1997.

[LM06]   Michele Lanza and Radu Marinescu. *Object-Oriented Metrics in Practice*. Springer, 2006.

[LP05]   W. Loewe and T. Panas. Rapid construction of software comprehension tools. In *Int'l Journal of Softw. Eng. and Knowledge Eng. 15(6)*, pages 905–1023, 2005.

[LRE03]   Michael D. Lee, Rachel E. Reilly, and Butavicius Marcus E. An empirical evaluation of chernoff faces, star glyphs, and spatial visualizations for binary data. In *Proc. Asia-Pacific Symp. on Info. visualisation*, pages 1–10, 2003.

[LRP95]   John Lamping, Ramana Rao, and Peter Pirolli. A focus+context technique based on hyperbolic geometry for visualizing large hierarchies. In *Proc. SIGCHI Conf. on Human factors in computing systems*, pages 401–408, 1995.

[Mar04a]   R. Marinescu. Detection strategies: metrics-based rules for detecting design flaws. In *Proc. IEEE Int'l Conf. on Softw. Maintenance*, pages 350–359, 2004.

[Mar04b]   Radu Marinescu. Detection strategies: Metrics-based rules for detecting design flaws. In *Proc. Int'l Conf. on Software Maintenance*, 2004.

[McC76]   Thomas J. McCabe. A complexity measure. *IEEE Trans. on Softw. Eng.*, 2(4), 1976.

[Meh82]   Nimish Mehta. *Flexible Machine Interface*. M.A.Sc. Thesis, Department of Electrical Engineering, University of Toronto supervised by Professor K.C. Smith, 1982.

[MFM03]   Andrian Marcus, Louis Feng, and Jonathan I. Maletic. 3d representations for software visualization. In *Proc. ACM Symp. on Softw. Visualization*, pages 27–36, 2003.

[MSR00]   Christopher J. Morris, Ebert David S., and Penny Rheingans. An experimental analysis of the effectiveness of features in chernoff faces. In *Proc. SPIE Conf. on Applied Imagery Pattern Recognition*, volume 3905, pages 12–17, 2000.

[MW01]   Russell Mosemann and Susan Wiedenbeck. Navigation and compre-
            hension of programs by novice programmers. In *Proc. Int'l Workshop
            on Program Comprehension*, page 79, 2001.

[NH02]   Quang Vinh Nguyen and Mao Lin Huang. A space-optimized tree
            visualization. *IEEE Symp. on Info. Visualization*, page 85, 2002.

[NR83]   L. H. Nakatani and John A. Rohrlich. Soft machines: A philosophy
            of user-computer interface design. In *Proc. of the ACM Conf. on
            Human Factors in Computing Systems (CHI83)*, pages 12–15, 1983.

[Ost07]   L. J. Osterweil. A future of software engineering? In *Proc. of Future
            of Software Engineering (FOSE)*, pages 1–11, 2007.

[Pac04]   Michael J. Pacione. Software visualisation for object-oriented pro-
            gram comprehension. In *Proc. Int'l Conf. on Softw. Eng.*, pages 63–
            65, 2004.

[Pen87a]   N. Pennington. Comprehension strategies in programming. In *In
            G. M. Olson, S. Sheppard & E. Soloway, Eds. Empirical Studies of
            Programmers: Second Workshop*, pages 100– 113, 1987.

[Pen87b]   N. Pennington. Stimulus structures and mental representations in ex-
            pert comprehension of computer programs. In *Cognitive Psychology*,
            pages 295–341, 1987.

[PEQ+07]   T. Panas, T. Epperly, D. Quinlan, A. Saebjornsen, and R. Vuduc.
            Communicating software architecture using a unified single-view vi-
            sualization. In *Proc. Int'l Conf. on Eng. Complex Computer Systems*,
            pages 217–228, 2007.

[PGFL05]   Martin Pinzger, Harald Gall, Michael Fischer, and Michele Lanza.
            Visualizing multiple evolution metrics. In *Proc. ACM Symp. on Softw.
            Visualization*, pages 67–75, 2005.

[Pin05]   Martin Pinzger. *ArchView - Analyzing Evolutionary Aspects of Com-
            plex Software Systems*. Vienna University of Technology, 2005.

[PMI07]   R. Pfeifer, Lungarella M., and F. Iida. Self-organization, embodi-
            ment, and biologically inspired robotics. In *Science 318*, pages 1088–
            1093, 2007.

[PRW03]   Michael J. Pacione, M. Roper, and M. Wood. A comparative eval-
           uation of dynamic visualisation tools. In *Proc. Working Conf. on
           Reverse Eng.*, pages 80–89, 2003.

[Ree79]   Trygve Reenskaug. Models - views - controllers. In *Technical report,
           Xerox Parc*, 1979.

[Rek02]   Jun Rekimoto. Smartskin: An infrastructure for freehand manipula-
           tion on interactive surfaces. In *Proc. of ACM SIGCHI*, 2002.

[RMC91]   George G. Robertson, Jock D. Mackinlay, and Stuart K. Card. Cone
           trees: animated 3d visualizations of hierarchical information. In
           Proc. SIGCHI Conf. on Human factors in computing systems, pages
           189–194, 1991.

[RMG06]   Gerald Reif, Martin Morger, and Harald C. Gall. Semantic Clipboard
           - Semantically Enriched Data Exchange Between Desktop Applica-
           tions. In *Semantic Desktop and Social Semantic Collaboration Work-
           shop at the 5th Int'l Semantic Web Conf. ISWC06*, page 13, Athens,
           Georgia, US, November 2006.

[RMK+05]   Mitchel Resnick, Brad Myers, Nakakoji Kumiyo, Ben Shneiderman,
           Randy Pausch, Ted Selker, and Mike Eisenberg. Design principles for
           tools to support creative thinking. In *Workshop on Creativity Support
           Tools*, pages 286–293, 2005.

[RRHT03]   Tom Rodden, Yvonne Rogers, John Halloran, and Ian Taylor. De-
           signing novel interactional workspaces to support face to face con-
           sultations. In *CHI '03: Proc. Conf. on Human factors in computing
           systems*, pages 57–64, 2003.

[SAPB07]   Andreas Stefik, Roger Alexander, Robert Patterson, and Jonathan
           Brown. Wad: A feasibility study using the wicked audio debugger.
           In *Proc. IEEE Int'l Conf. on Program Comprehension*, pages 69–80,
           2007.

[SB94]   Manojit Sarkar and Marc H. Brown. Graphical fisheye views. *Com-
           mun. ACM*, 37(12):73–83, 1994.

[SBD99]   Jason Stewart, Benjamin B. Bederson, and Allison Druin. Single
           display groupware: a model for co-present collaboration. In *CHI '99:
           Proc. Conf. on Human factors in computing systems*, pages 286–293,
           1999.

[SBM⁺02]   Margaret-Anne Storey, Casey Best, Jeff Michaud, Derek Rayside, Marin Litoiu, and Mark Musen. Shrimp views: an interactive environment for information visualization and navigation. In *Extended abstracts SIGCHI Conf. on Human factors in computing systems*, pages 520–521, 2002.

[SFM98]   M. A. D. Storey, F. D. Fracchia, and H. A. Mueller. Cognitive design elements to support the construction of a mental model during software exploration. In *The Journal of System and Software 44 p. 171-185*, pages 171–185, 1998.

[She07]   Chia Shen. *From Clicks to Touches: Enabling Face-to-Face Shared Social Interface on Multi-touch Tabletops*. Springer, 2007.

[SKCC10]   Gwenda L. Schmidt, Alexander Kranjec, Eileen R. Cardillo, and Anjan Chatterjee. Beyond laterality: A critical assessment of research on the neural basis of metaphor. In *Journal of the International Neuropsychological Society (16)*, pages 1–5, 2010.

[SMV06]   Jonathan Sillito, Gail C. Murphy, and Kris De Volder. Questions programmers ask during software evolution tasks. In *Proc. SIGSOFT Foundations of Softw. Eng. Conf. (FSE)*, 2006.

[SMV07]   Jonathan Sillito, Gail C. Murphy, and Kris De Volder. Asking and answering questions during a programming change task. In *Transactions of Softw. Eng.*, 2007.

[SVFM05]   Jonathan Sillito, Kris De Volder, Brian Fisher, and Gail C. Murphy. Managing software change tasks: An exploratory study. In *Proc. Int'l Symposium on Emirical Softw. Eng.*, 2005.

[TH99]   Edward R. Tufte and G. Howard. *The Visual Display of Quantitative Information*. Graphics Press, 1999.

[VA96]   Paul Vickers and James. L Alty. Caitlin: A musical program auralization tool to assist novice programmers with debugging. In *Proc. Int'l Conf. on Auditory Display*, 1996.

[VA03]   Paul Vickers and James. L Alty. Siren songs and swan songs: Debugging with music. In *Commun. ACM 46, 7*, pages 86–92, 2003.

[VDC90]   E. Vuorio and B. De Crombrugghe. The family of collagen genes. In *Annual review of biochemistry, 1990*, 1990.

[Vic04]   Paul Vickers. External auditory representations of programs: Past, present, and future—an aesthetic perspective. In *Proc. Int'l Conf. on Auditory Display*, 2004.

[VW05]   M. C. Vigeant and L. M. Wang. Subjective evaluation of auralizations created from multi-channel anechoic recordings of a talker in motion. *Acoustical Society of America Journal*, 117:2465–2465, apr 2005.

[Whi07]   Jim Whitehead. Collaboration in software engineering: A roadmap. In *FOSE '07: 2007 Future of Software Engineering*, 2007.

[WL07]   Richard Wettel and Michele Lanza. Program comprehension through software habitability. In *Proc. Int'l Conf. on Program Comprehension*, 2007.

[WL08]   Richard Wettel and Michele Lanza. Codecity. In *Proc. Int'l Workshop on Advanced Software Development Tools and Techniques (WAS-DeTT 2008)*, 2008.

[Yin94]   Robert K. Yin. *Case Study Research - Design and methods*. Sage Publications, 1994.

[YWR02a]   Jing Yang, M. O. Ward, and E. A. Rundensteiner. Interring: an interactive tool for visually navigating and manipulating hierarchical structures. pages 77–84, 2002.

[YWR02b]   Jing Yang, Matthew O. Ward, and Elke A. Rundensteiner. Interring: An interactive tool for visually navigating and manipulating hierarchical structures. In *IEEE Symposium on Information Visualization*, page 77, 2002.

[ZFH01]   E. Zwicker, H. Fastl, and W. M. Hartmann. "psychoacoustics: Facts and models". *Physics Today*, 54:64–65, 2001.

Curriculum Vitae

Name: Sandro Boccuzzo
Nationality: Switzerland and Italy
Date of Birth: December 22, 1977
Place of Birth: Zurich , Switzerland

Education

2006-2012 Doctoral Study in Informatics at the Software Evolution and Architecture Lab, Department of Informatics, University of Zurich, Switzerland

Advisor: Prof. Dr. Harald C. Gall
External Examiner: Prof. Dr. Michele Lanza

2004-2009 IT Auditor and Consultant for Deloitte AG Enterprise Risk Services Department.

1999-2004 Master in computer science with concentration in information systems and business informatics at the University of Zurich, Switzerland

Master thesis: 'Data mining in Weka and Mining Mart' Advisor: Prof. Dr. Abraham Bernstein

1995-1999 Kantonschule Oerlikon in Zurich, Switzerland

1984-1995 Primary School in Zurich, Switzerland

www.ingramcontent.com/pod-product-compliance
Lightning Source LLC
Chambersburg PA
CBHW071424050326
40689CB00010B/1977